Money in Motion

A Back to Basics Approach
to Build Your Business

Doug E. Lachance

www.backtobasicscoach.com

Note for Librarians: A cataloguing record for this book is available from Library and Archives Canada at www.collectionscanada.ca/amicus/index-e.html
ISBN 1-4120-6694-8

Printed in Victoria, BC, Canada. Printed on paper with minimum 30% recycled fibre. Trafford's print shop runs on "green energy" from solar, wind and other environmentally-friendly power sources.

TRAFFORD
PUBLISHING

Offices in Canada, USA, Ireland and UK
This book was published *on-demand* in cooperation with Trafford Publishing. On-demand publishing is a unique process and service of making a book available for retail sale to the public taking advantage of on-demand manufacturing and Internet marketing. On-demand publishing includes promotions, retail sales, manufacturing, order fulfilment, accounting and collecting royalties on behalf of the author.

Book sales for North America and international:
Trafford Publishing, 6E–2333 Government St.,
Victoria, BC v8t 4p4 CANADA
phone 250 383 6864 (toll-free 1 888 232 4444)
fax 250 383 6804; email to orders@trafford.com
Book sales in Europe:
Trafford Publishing (uk) Limited, 9 Park End Street, 2nd Floor
Oxford, UK ox1 1hh UNITED KINGDOM
phone 44 (0)1865 722 113 (local rate 0845 230 9601)
facsimile 44 (0)1865 722 868; info.uk@trafford.com
Order online at:
trafford.com/05-1605

10 9 8 7 6 5 4 3

Money in Motion

A Back to Basics Approach
to Build Your Business

www.backtobasicscoach.com

ACKNOWLEDGEMENTS

There are a number of people I would like to thank who helped make this book possible.

First of all, my co-workers at Pemberton Securities. Not only did this firm give me a chance to be an Investment Advisor, working with everyone there was a lot of fun and I have some great memories of this incredible firm. In particular, a special thanks to Ivan Moldowan who believed in me and gave me advice, support and guidance in the early years.

I would like to thank National Bank Financial for giving me the freedom to write Money in Motion and create the "Back to Basics Coach". Special thanks to Germain, Luc, Benoit, Richard, Gordon, Christine and Stephan and everyone else at NBF.

Thank you also to all the other wonderful people I've worked with over the years, and to everyone else who's paths I've crossed and who in one way or another helped me along the way.

Thanks also to Evelyn Jacks for her support, guidance and unwavering belief in me. You really helped the book evolve and be as good as it could be.

In addition, thanks to Cyndy for the many hours she spent in proofing the manuscript and providing some suggestions to make it better.

Finally, thank you to my lovely wife Gina, who endured countless rewrites over the five years it took to finally publish the book. Thanks Hon! What would I do without you.

Doug E. Lachance
November, 2005

TABLE OF CONTENTS

Find out how I discovered a prospecting system that took me to President's Club production with 3 separate clientele's. See how a good work ethic combined with a commitment to a process and methodology works in any and every sales, business development, or fund raising activity.

What is a 'Money in Motion' event?

What are the events unique to your business that cause people to buy your product or move their business to you? Find out how to identify these moments and how to position yourself with your prospects to get an opportunity to present your value proposition when this time comes.

Have you ever thought about why you choose a product or service?

How does a need evolve into a decision to choose someone new to do business with? What are the reasons why someone might choose you?

Stranger ⇨ Acquaintance ⇨ Trust ⇨ Need ⇨ Customer

People do business with those they trust. Learn how to gently position yourself for the moment when 'Money Goes in Motion'.

Do you know what the 3 Steps are to land a new customer?

Find out how to move your relationships forward, with a pipeline of people just like your best customers, so new business opportunities are regularly presented to you.

Wouldn't it be great to have a pipeline of prospects who have the potential to be one of your best customers?

Let me show you how to build a pipeline of people moving towards the day when they will want to do business with you.

Are you ready to go?

Here is what you need to be thinking about if you want to be ready for the new business opportunities that are about to happen for you.

Have you ever closed your eyes, took a deep breath, and took a step into the unknown?

Learn how to focus on measurable results that will translate into new business opportunities. Be inspired to believe enough, not to give up, to dig deep, and force yourself to continue to make the effort.

How good a job do you do for your customers?

Find out how to inject conviction and passion into all you do, to result in more productive conversations and meetings.

Do you know the secret of converting good ideas into action?

Discover how to use projects to be more productive. See how they can create an energy of their own, and how to organize, and prioritize, all the things that need to be done.

Do you think you can block everything out for an hour or two?

Learn how the power of a focused effort results in your accomplishing more things in less time.

Do you want it bad enough?

Let me show you how to set achievable goals, how to use Call Sheets, and a reward system, to end each week with positive results.

How would you like to be meeting people who already know you, trust you, and are ready to do business with you?

Here are the strategies you can use to create customer advocates who are constantly telling everyone about you.

How can you find more people just like your best customers?

Let me help you define your ideal customer, and show you the sources, and strategies, available to find more people just like them.

*What are you prepared to do
to help your prospects get to know you better?*

Learn how to create a powerful "slow drip" that will build trust and familiarity.

How do you meet someone who has no interest in meeting you?

Let me show you how to use seminars and networking activities to meet your best prospects, and others just like them.

*How would you like to belong to a club
exclusively comprised of your best customers and their peers?*

Let me show you how reading a book entitled "Selling to the Affluent" by Thomas J. Stanley, inspired me to create a networking group compromised exclusively of people who had the potential to be my best customers. "SUCCESS" was chosen as one of "The Great Ideas" from Top Performers.

What would you like to know about this person?

Find out how to prepare for a meeting, control the meeting, and how to plant the seeds **and get a commitment** for a new business opportunity.

Are you ready to inject some new energy into your business? For the next 3 months implement the systems and processes discussed in this book and use the following forms to assist you in doing so.

A list of some websites that you might find helpful.

FOREWORD

MY JOURNEY

By
Doug E. Lachance

I began my career in the investment industry on December 15th, 1979 with Pemberton Securities. Over the next 25 years, due to changes in my personal life, I built three separate books of clients. Each of these clienteles took me to the President's Club every year (recognition of the top 25% of producers in the company).

Prior to coming into the investment business, I spent 5 years with the Canadian Imperial Bank of Commerce, transferring 13 times during the booming 70's. The bank was my University. While there, I learned a little bit about many things: personnel, accounting, administration, time management, organization, supervision, business writing, marketing, and business development.

My last position with the bank was Accountant, Main Branch, Calgary. This was the second most senior administrative post in Alberta. It was a more senior posting than that of manager in many small branches. Even so, my salary was very low due to salary administration policies. After discovering I had some abilities, I yearned to work in a career where my income would equal those abilities, where there would be no ceiling on what I could make if I was good at it.

I knew absolutely nothing about the stock market. I did not know what the Dow Jones Industrial Average or the TSE 300 was. All I knew was that "stockbrokers" made a lot of money.

In 1979 when I applied for a job in the investment industry, things were a lot different than they are now. Stockbrokers were stockbrokers. Mutual Funds were virtually unknown. Investors were quite unsophisticated. If you did not own stocks, you would not think of yourself as an investor, regardless of how much money you had. There were those that owned stocks—and those that did not. For many of those who did own stocks, they were gamblers not investors. Howe Street was rife with promotions and promoters.

I was extremely fortunate to be hired by Pemberton Securities. Pemberton's was an old, highly respected firm that, unknown to me, had a great reputation for the quality of its people and it's advisor-training program.

As I walked through the huge bullpen for my first interview and looked at all of the stockbrokers on the phones, I can remember thinking, "These are just people. I'm as good as they are!". Although I had this vision of them being so different and special, they were just people. Moreover, I can remember thinking, "If they can do it, so can I!".

Pemberton's had a great training program. They believed that success was achieved by developing quality relationships and building a quality asset base. They were very early in realizing that a growing asset base would result in a growing revenue stream.

I built my first clientele at Pemberton's. I did so without really knowing what I was doing from an Investment perspective, but believed in "The System" and executed it with an effort that would ensure that if I did not succeed it would be because of a flaw in the system, and not from any deficiency on my part.

And the system worked! Over the five-year period I was in Penticton, B.C., I built a clientele that led me to achieve the Presidents Council that recognized the top 20 brokers in the firm.

After 5 years building my first clientele, I decided I needed a change. I gave my business away and moved to White Rock to build a second clientele from scratch.

In 1984, White Rock was a quiet retirement community nestled on Semiahmoo Bay on the border of Blaine, Washington. I once again applied the same fundamental principles, and built a second clientele.

Over the next five years, this clientele once again took me to Presidents Club recognition. During this period, I changed firms and brought many of my clients with me. I decided in 1989 to make a change in my career path, gave away my second clientele, and left the industry for almost 2 years.

It was very interesting to be on the other side of the fence, however, the opportunity didn't work out as I had hoped. I had stayed connected to friends in the business during this time, and began to hear of some incredible numbers being put up. I thought, "What was I thinking?". I decided to go back into the investment industry.

I came back to the investment business in 1991. I went back to the same company I left on their condition that I could have any of my old clients back as they had been re-allotted and new relationships formed. I proceeded to build my third clientele, which over the next 10 years took me to production levels of over $1 million and of assets over $100 million.

I have now transitioned this third clientele to try some other things. I know that, if necessary, I could build another clientele and that I will always be able to achieve a very nice income. What a great thing to take with you through life!

That is not to say it's easy. It's hard. Really hard! You cannot give up. You must believe. You have to believe that if you continue to apply some basic fundamental principles and processes that, from this exercise, on the other side, the clientele will be there—and the income, security and lifestyle that goes with it.

I hope that I am able to help some of you be the success that you know you could be if you only had a roadmap.

This is my roadmap.

Good Luck!

CHAPTER 1

MONEY IN MOTION

What is a 'Money in Motion' event?

What are the events unique to your business that cause people to buy your product or move their business to you? How do you position yourself so that you are one of the providers they seriously consider when they have decided to do something? Find out how to identify these moments and how to position yourself with your prospects to get an opportunity to present your value proposition when this time comes. Let me show you how to use these opportunities to go head to head with your competition without them even knowing that they are in a competition, and how to land a new customer when your competition drops the ball.

Kick Start Checklist

✓ What are the 'Money in Motion' events unique to your business?
✓ How are you going to position yourself for when 'Money goes in Motion'?

CHAPTER 1

MONEY IN MOTION

The goal of building a great pipeline is to provide a steady stream of presentation opportunities. You have worked hard to position yourself with someone who is providing you with an opportunity to present your value proposition with an honest desire to hear what you have to say and to act on it if they like what you have to offer.

Your opportunity arises when 'Money goes in Motion'. In the investment business, many events can trigger this: selling a company; being fired and receiving a retirement allowance; receiving an inheritance or an event that acts as a catalyst for an existing investor to be interested in looking at a change. The event could be as simply as you calling them. Depending on the product or service you have to offer 'Money In Motion' could be triggered by many things; the birth of a child; a new partner; a death in the family; an unexpected bonus; dissatisfaction with their present provider.

Whatever has created this desire or need for change, if you are positioned with this person you have now been given an opportunity to land a new customer.

These opportunities become more and more frequent as your pipeline grows and matures. Hopefully, the day will come when most of your time is spent doing presentations to potential new customers.

I have discovered over the years in the investment industry that when it comes to their investments most people don't enjoy dealing with their money. If everything seems okay, many aren't prepared to put the effort into reviewing it. An event needs to occur, such as new money that forces them to think about it, or concerns about how their existing money is being managed. Whatever it is you have to offer, it has to be the right time for them to want to think about this area of their life. You must be gentle in your approach. When the time comes that they have a need, recognize it, and want to deal with it, you want this person to remember you and to be one of the proposals they consider.

When you are given an opportunity to analyze a person's situation and to provide them with your ideas and strategy, you must have a Value Proposition and an effective way of presenting it. If you do, you stand a very good chance of landing a new customer. They have come to trust you; they are seriously interested in what you have to offer and your value proposition. This does not necessarily mean the business will be immediately yours. This happens some of the time, but often not immediately. If it is new money, or a decision to change has been made, your proposal must be the best of the proposals being considered. Many times when 'Money goes in Motion' a prospect will arrange an interview with 2 or 3 providers. You are only one of a number of proposals they are considering. Your presentation and template must be powerful enough that, when given the opportunity to go head to head for the money, you and your strategy are the one chosen.

If the prospective customer is not ready to do business with you yet, but is seriously interested in what you have to offer, you now have an opportunity to go head to head with whomever they are currently dealing with. Many times your competition is unaware they are even in a competition! You have an excellent opportunity to land a new customer if the relationship is weak, or the service and/or performance unsatisfactory! At the very least, you will give the person something to think about and the beginnings of a new way of looking at their existing provider and level of service. At some point, something will happen. Your competition will drop the ball and Boom!, you have a new customer.

It's a great day when you land a new customer. It is the culmination of a lot of work. One of the nicest things though is that by the time you finally land the customer most of the work is already done. You simply update key information and execute—a great day!

A. HOW DO YOU IDENTIFY WHEN MONEY WILL GO IN MOTION?

As I mentioned previously, depending on your product or service there could be a number of life events that could act as a trigger for someone to look seriously at what you have to offer. Think about what the events are in your industry. In the insurance business, it could be the birth or death of a family member. Do you know this person and are you connected well enough that you will be aware of this event?

It's easy to see that the better the information you have about a prospective customer's life and family the better positioned you will be when the life event happens that creates a need for your services.

You must position yourself with this person. When the next time comes that 'Money goes in Motion' for your product or service, you want to be sure you are one of the ones being offered the opportunity to fill their need. The goal of building a pipeline is to have a pool of people putting you on their short list when they have a need for your product or service. You accomplish this by having a very methodical system in place to: capture potential new customers; meet them; "slow drip" them; build a relationship; and position yourself for the time when they are ready to become your customer.

"The surest way to be in position to get an opportunity when someone's need arises is to be connecting with this person on a regular basis."

B. EXAMPLES OF 'Money In Motion' EVENTS

Depending on your service or business, many different things can trigger a 'Money in Motion' event. Following are some examples of these for a few different types of services or businesses:

Doug E. Lachance

INVESTMENT ADVISORS

- Inheritance
- Divorce
- Lottery
- Lawsuit
- Relocation
- Death
- Bonuses
- Dividends (Private Co..)
- Redemptions
- Retractions

- IPO
- Severance
- Monetization
- Option Exercise
- Sale of Business or Real Estate
- Mergers & Acquisitions
- Conversion
- Maturity
- Retirement
- RSP Contribution

FINANCIAL PLANNERS

- Inheritance
- Divorce
- Lottery
- Lawsuit
- Relocation
- Death

- Retirement
- Severance
- RSP Contribution
- Sale of Business or Real Estate
- Dividends (Private Co..)
- Bonuses

MORTGAGE BROKERS

- Mortgage Maturing
- Commercial Real Estate Transactions
- Obtaining a Second Mortgage for:
  - Upgrades
  - Renovations
- Life Events:
  - Marriage
  - Financial Stress
  - Divorce

- Buying a Home

- Buying a Business

  - Liquidity
  - Lifestyle Benefits

BANKER

- Marriage
- Relocation
- Mortgage Maturing

- Retirement
- Birth/Death

- Obtaining a Second Mortgage for:
  - Upgrades
  - Renovations
- Commercial Loans for:
  - Real Estate
  - Business Expansion

- Liquidity
- Lifestyle Benefits

- Buying a new business

INSURANCE SPECIALISTS - PERSONAL
- Birth
- Divorce
- Promotion
- Family Illness
- Taxes

- Marriage
- New Job
- Retirement
- Income Needs

INSURANCE SPECIALISTS - BUSINESS
- New Partner or Owner
- Business Succession
- Growth
- Taxes

- Buy/Sell Agreement
- Estate Freeze
- Expansion

REALTOR
- Marriage
- Children Coming
- Children Going
- Divorce
- Death
- Relocation

- Promotion
- Sale of Business
- Expansion of Business
- Downsizing
- Retirement

AUTO SALES ASSOCIATE
- Lease Expiring
- Bonus
- Raise
- Promotion
- New Job

- Inheritance
- Lottery
- New Baby
- Asset Sale: House, Business, etc.

CHAPTER 2

THE EVOLUTION OF A SALE

Have you ever thought about why you choose a product or service?

What is it that causes us to decide to buy something? Once the decision has been made, what is the process that we follow to get what we're after? How do we choose whom we will get it from? What are the reasons why someone might buy from you? Find out how important it is to position yourself for new opportunities and how to turn those opportunities into new customers.

Kick Start Checklist

✓ Why do you choose a product or service?
✓ What is the process to land a new customer in your business?

CHAPTER 2

THE EVOLUTION OF A SALE

What is it that causes someone to become a new customer? What are the ingredients of the decision making process? It will be something the person wants or needs. They must believe that this is the time to get it, or do it, and they must have the financial capability to do so.

It could be they are actively seeking someone who does what you do. Some event in their life could have acted as a catalyst and energized them to take action. It could also be something they have been thinking about for some time, and now that you have positioned yourself in such a way, it is only natural for them to get it done. Alternatively, the initial introduction perhaps was powerful enough that it acted as the catalyst itself and the sale or close naturally flowed from there.

Whatever combination of events has resulted in the purchase event to occur, once the decision has been made, the only other decision is to decide whom to work with to satisfy this need. There are many ways you may have been chosen to be given consideration to be the provider. Perhaps one of your existing customers referred this person to you; perhaps you cold called them once and they became part of your pipeline and the relationship has grown; perhaps they heard about you from some other source, event, or activity. Somehow, from whatever the source, you are one of the chosen to show your value proposition.

What is it that is going to cause this person to choose you, whether you are the only choice, or one of many? It will be because they trust you, and your presentation made them believe that you are the best person, with the best solution to a perceived need, at a price they feel is fair and reasonable.

There is a process to the evolution of a sale. First, there must be a need. It does not matter how good you are or how wonderful your product or service is, if the person you are talking to does not presently have a need for it, there will not be a sale. Sometimes you will discover that they do have a need, but they are unwilling to do anything about it because they do not perceive the need to be great enough to do anything about it currently. At whatever time it is that the person decides to meet this need, whom are they going to select to fulfill their need? Most of the time it will be someone that they trust—someone they have come to know, or were referred to by somebody they trust.

When I think back to the times I have made a major purchase decision, I realize that in all of those decisions, the person I bought from was very influential in the process. I trusted them and as I recall, I liked them. In some instances they were there when I decided to do something, and managed my decision making process well enough to land me as a customer. In others, the relationship and my trust in them grew until the time came when I had a need and then they were the natural candidate to meet this need. Sometimes, someone I knew referred me to them. I wanted to do business with them. I felt that it was good for them as well as being good for me, and was glad I was doing business with them.

Sometimes, one person was the catalyst, but I then brought someone that I trusted into the process and they got the business. No matter how the person came into the picture, the one I did business with was always the one I thought would do the best job for me.

I have always found that making a decision to change a service provider was always a positive event for me. Regardless whether the event that triggered this action was positive or negative, it was a new beginning. New beginnings are always positive. Sometimes they are positive because this purchase decision is something you have wanted to do for some time, and you're excited about finally doing it. Perhaps a bad experience triggered you taking this action. Although motivated by a negative experience, the action of replacement is a positive experience. It's a new beginning and bad memories are now left behind.

Just as I have always been happy to find a new service provider, and relieved when it was done, so too will your new customers. You will have managed the presentation process in such a way that all doubts have been removed. This person trusts and believes that you are exactly the right person, with exactly the right solution at the right price, and when they sign the final papers, they are going to breathe a sigh or relief that the decision is over, and then smile upon reflecting on the positive experience of making the right choice.

"You need to manage this process for them!"

First, you must position yourself—you must be one of the providers chosen to present a value proposition.

When given the opportunity you must shine—and you will! Your presentation will be the one they choose because it will have all the ingredients necessary and one more that none of the others have—you!

Just as you feel great when you buy a new product or service, so too will your new customer. They came to know you, trust you, believe in you, and now look forward to working with you for a long time to come. (Of course, at this time you are going to ask them if they have a friend whom you might also be of service to.)

CHAPTER 3

THE RELATIONSHIP CURVE

Stranger ⇨ *Acquaintance* ⇨ *Trust* ⇨ *Need* ⇨ *Customer*

People do business with those they trust. Learn how to build trust with people and how to position yourself with them for the time when they have a need for your product or service. Find out about the Relationship Curve; how relationships change with time; how trust grows, and how one day this growing trust usually results in a presentation opportunity. Learn how to gently position yourself for the moment when your product or service is needed—when 'Money Goes in Motion'.

Kick Start Checklist

✓ What is your game plan to build trust with the people who have the potential to be your best customers?
✓ Where are your existing prospects on the Relationship Curve?
✓ How are you planning to move people along the Relationship Curve?

CHAPTER 3

THE RELATIONSHIP CURVE

A. HOW A RELATIONSHIP GROWS

When you first target someone on a contact list, they are a Stranger. When you contact and qualify them, they become an Acquaintance and a prospect. As time goes by, Trust grows. Then one day 'Money goes in Motion'. They have a Need for your product or service. They sell their business; inherit money; become dissatisfied with their present provider, or an event occurs and Boom! The presentation opportunity comes and you seize the moment. They become your Customer. This is the process. Although very simple, it takes time and you must be committed to the long-term. Building a clientele is a 3 to 5 year project for the foundation and over 5 years to produce the big numbers. 5 years is a long time. The little things that you do every day can have a huge impact when done for 3 to 5 years, and then 5 to10 years, or more.

"Relationships Change Over Time!"

It is amazing how a relationship changes over time. Even if you have met someone in person, or especially if you haven't. It is really something when you have been calling someone for 2 or 3 years (or even 5 or more) and still have not met them, and still have not gone away. They can't believe it! They gain a great respect for your persistence.

Doug E. Lachance

Many times early in my clientele building, as I have hung up from someone who was not interested at the time, I had thought to myself, "I wonder what they're going to think when I'm still calling 5 years from now?"

If it was obvious this person was not interested at the time, I hung up and made a diary note for 3 months to call again. Over a five-year period, that's only 20 calls of 2 or 3 minutes each. Is this person worth an hour of your time every 5 years?

During the building of my clienteles, I was the primary caller. Over the years, I have been fortunate to find on occasion, a young student who is very sharp and productive. These people are hard to find, and when you do find them, must be cherished. I enjoy talking to people on the phone, and like everyone, I prefer warm calls to cold. It is critical you are consistently talking to and meeting people. If you do not like cold calling then you must build a team and a business model that will make new contacts happen and result in your being able to exclusively make warm calls or have meetings with people.

Somehow, somebody has to be making first contact with people, creating warm calls for you and building your pipeline.

Most of the time however, the process moves along more quickly. I only want to emphasize the importance of thinking long term. As time goes by you will no longer be a stranger. There becomes a familiarity to your relationship. They may not know you; they may not have met you; but you are slowly becoming familiar to them and their respect for you is growing. You are the one who doesn't give up! The one who will not go away! They come to admire your persistence if it is gentle and truly has their interests and a long-term relationship in mind. You prove that you believe in long-term relationships by making this a long-term relationship even though the person has not done any business with you or given you any encouragement to continue to hang in there; call after call, month after month, year after year.

Moreover, one day they will meet you. And one day they will trust you, and then become your customer. My personal record to land a client is 14 years. I prospected him through the building of two clienteles.

B. RELATIONSHIPS MUST GROW TO BE HARVESTED

Trust is arguably the single most important ingredient in having someone become your customer. When they have reached a point where, for whatever reason, they are looking for someone new, you will have built up sufficient trust for them to give your product or service serious consideration. You must capitalize on this opportunity. We will talk about that later but first, you must position yourself to get the opportunity.

Many times, when you end the conversation from the first contact, the person immediately forgets about you. It is a long journey from this complete unfamiliarity to a place where they know who you are, know what you do, and trust you enough to give you an opportunity to do a presentation to show them what you can do.

This is where the pipeline kicks in. After you make the first contact with them, you are not going to go away until **You** decide its time to sever the relationship.

You are about to "slow drip" them, and as time goes by they will come to know you, respect you, trust you, and one day become your customer.

C. FEELING A RELATIONSHIP GROW

It is a wonderful feeling to feel a relationship grow. A new tone of voice; a higher level of intimacy and confidentially; you can feel the warmth.

It is noticeable in the conversation. As time goes by, it is wonderful the way you can feel the distance of a stranger move towards the closeness of a friend.

The day comes when the person recognizes your name; is familiar with your voice; is more and more comfortable with you as a part of their life, albeit a very small part, but growing all the time.

They may not want to become your customer yet; or even meet you; they may not want to accelerate the relationship at this point, but the beginning of a long-term relationship has occurred. It is almost magical how the relationship grows and changes over time.

D. THE CHANGING SITUATION

Life is not static. Everything is constantly changing. So too is everyone's life. Things happen. People come into money. Whoever is presently providing their service or product can make a change or retire. Perhaps your prospect will become unhappy with their present provider. Sometimes a support person can drop the ball on the administration side. Whatever the catalyst suddenly, unexpectedly, the person is ready to seriously look at other possibilities and consider a change. And you will be there. Because of his previous provider not being able to execute a wire transfer in a timely manner for him, I landed my largest account ever. It was the catalyst that caused him to make a change.

When the opportunity finally comes, the person is often ready to give serious consideration what you have to offer. They wouldn't give you the opportunity otherwise. The trust is there.

This person, after whatever period of time, has gained a sufficient level of trust to provide you with the information you need to do a detailed analysis of their situation, and to give you an opportunity to present your product or service. They are ready to become your customer. All you need to do is land them.

E. TIME

I cannot emphasize enough the importance of a long-term perspective. When you make your first call to someone, it is difficult to imagine talking to him or her for years without actually doing business with them.

One thing I have discovered from building these clienteles is "time goes by". To have a process where you call someone at least a couple of times a year, where they receive information regularly, is not a time consuming thing to do.

Moreover, the years do fly by. No matter how you use your time, the years fly by. If you have a systematic methodology to your prospecting, time flying by will become your friend. Each time you call someone and they are still not ready to meet or do business with you, they are that much further down the road of a long-term relationship. Their respect for your persistence and long-term thinking is growing. As the years fly by your small connection naturally grows into and becomes a long-term relationship.

F. YOU HAVE TO BE A LONG-TERM THINKER

What do you think the probability is that the very first time you call someone:

1. They will be ready to change their service provider right at that moment after probably having a relationship with the person for many years.
2. They will want to transfer all their business to you immediately, a person they have never known or talked to before in their life—a complete stranger!

"Not Likely!"

Incredibly this sometimes happens. Rarely, but on occasion, you will call exactly the right person, at exactly the right moment in time. This is a beautiful thing but unfortunately, it does not happen very often.

More often, the person will not even be interested in talking to you. It could even be someone who is quite unhappy with his or her current provider, your competition. They just are not thinking about it at that moment in time when you call, and are not in the mood to do so at that moment.

There is a distance to travel from the first contact to the day they are ready to tell you everything about their situation. A ways to go before you can then convince them during the Analysis and Proposal presentation that they should hire you.

Relationships take time to grow. In fact, that is what a relationship is—TIME! We measure relationships in increments of time. As time goes by, there is a change in a relationship that can be felt and observed. "How long have you known each other?" is one of our most cherished relationship values.

It is at this point that the relationship has reached the right level of trust and 'Money goes in Motion' that an opportunity will present itself.

"You seize the moment!"

How often do you instantly trusted someone you have just met, someone whom you have never heard of before? Not often! Trust takes time to grow.

"How well would you have to know someone
to give them your business?"

G. MOVING PEOPLE ALONG THE RELATIONSHIP CURVE

Where are your prospects at on the relationship curve? Make a list of all the people that are in your pipeline. Determine the position of each of them on the relationship curve. What can you do to move them along? Look at each name. When did you last speak to them? Should you send them something? What can you do to build on your relationship? Call them and arrange to get together with them? Perhaps you could send them a handwritten note.

I found it very valuable once every 3 months to go completely through my pipeline, name by name, card by card (or by whatever system you are using to record notes and comments). Ideas would always pop into my head for a good number of people: "This person should be invited to my seminar or open house." "I know a great article this person would enjoy." "Gosh, I haven't spoken to this person for some time now. Maybe I should give them a call." And so on. The important thing is that you review your pipeline regularly.

"Look for ways to move people along the relationship curve."

Maybe they are closer to becoming a customer than you think!

H. REFERRALS

Referrals are a great way to instantly move someone to the end of the pipeline process. Now presented to you is an opportunity that might take years for you to obtain otherwise. 'Money in Motion' and a level of trust are already in place. For these opportunities (and all others of course), you must have a presentation template that will deliver them to you as a customer. I discuss this later.

You must always be searching for referral opportunities. Asking new customers; building relationships with centers of influence; having a great relationship with your existing customers so that they are motivated to refer family and friends to you.

There are many coaches and systems devoted entirely to service and relationship building with existing customers to generate referrals. Whichever system you use to get referrals from your existing customer base, it should be a very important part of your business plan. Remember:

"Never stop asking for referrals!"

This is absolute the warmest presentation opportunity that exists. Establish a discipline for asking for referrals. As your customer base grows, referrals will one day become your entire source of new business (Won't that be nice!).

** *Please refer to Chapter 12—How to Get Your Best Customers to Refer Their Family and Friends to You.*

CHAPTER 4

THE 3 FUNDAMENTAL STEPS TO LANDING A NEW CUSTOMER

Do you know what the 3 steps are to land a new customer?

If you would like to build a pipeline full of people who are just like your best customers, and move these relationships forward so opportunities are being presented regularly, you must understand the process. Discover the 3 steps to land a customer. Learn how to identify and capture new people for your pipeline. Learn the importance of meeting people and building the relationship for the moment when 'Money goes in Motion' and you land a new customer. You will find out how to build and manage an ever-growing pipeline of quality people moving towards the day they become your customer.

Kick Start Checklist

✓   What are the 3 Steps to land new customers?

CHAPTER 4

THE 3 FUNDAMENTAL STEPS TO LANDING A NEW CUSTOMER

I believe there are 3 fundamental steps to converting people to customers. They are:

1. Introducing Yourself—Identify and capture the person for your pipeline.
2. Building a Relationship and Positioning Yourself—Moving the person along the relationship curve until they trust you and are ready to do business with you.
3. Landing a new Customer when 'Money goes in Motion'— Having a presentation that lands the customer every time.

Think about any one of your customers. How and when did you meet them? Were they a referral? How did they become your prospect? How did you qualify them? Did they become your customer right away? Did you feel the relationship change after you met them for the first time? Were they ready to see your presentation immediately or did this opportunity come later? When were they ready to become your customer, and how did you make that happen?

With every one of your customers the above three steps will have happened. Somehow, you were introduced to each other. Over time, from a few hours to many months or years, they came to know you and understand what you do and to trust you. At the same time you gained a detailed look at their situation and came to know what you could do for them and when. At some point, they were ready to see your presentation. You delivered it and they liked what they saw enough to either right then, or later, do what you recommended for them and became your customer.

So, if that is how it always works, why doesn't it work like that all the time? Let us look at some of the obstacles that stand in the way.

1. Introducing Yourself—Identify and capture the person for your pipeline.

The first obstacle and the one that stops the whole process dead in its tracks is not introducing yourself to new people who have the potential to become great customers. For growth to happen you absolutely must introduce yourself to some new qualified prospects. (This is discussed in more detail later.) Finding or creating a list; calling yourself or hiring someone to call for you; holding seminars or events and encouraging your best customers to invite their family and friends; advertising or other promotional activities. Somehow, one way or another you need new prospects to go into your pipeline.

2. Building a Relationship and Positioning Yourself—Moving the person along the relationship curve until they trust you enough to be ready to do business with you.

I have previously discussed the relationship curve. At the end of this curve is the day you are presented with the opportunity to show your presentation to someone who is ready to be your customer. The starting point is different with every new person. Capturing a cold called stranger for your pipeline can be difficult. Many of them have their defenses up, and it can be difficult to break through. If they do not have a present need for you, they will make every effort to get rid of you. There is no motivation whatsoever to start a relationship with you. Warm prospects that have come to you are easier to capture for your pipeline. With these prospects, it is more a matter of qualifying them and waiting for the 'Money in Motion' opportunity.

Depending how they have come into your pipeline will determine where they are on the relationship curve. Some will be ready to see your presentation and become your customer. Many will not be ready for this and you will need to determine where they are on the relationship curve. You will need to work hard to build trust and position yourself for the day when they are ready to become your customer.

After the initial introduction, and your choice to capture this person into your pipeline, now you must somehow find a way to meet them. Possibly, they have agreed to meet you, or they are participating in an event you are a part of or hosting. Perhaps you are still looking for other ways to break through. Regardless, you must meet them somehow. However this meeting happens, once they meet you, you will become a person to them. Other than the moment of capturing someone for your pipeline, this is the most important point on the relationship curve. From this moment on, you are positioning yourself for that moment in time when this person is ready to become your customer.

Positioning. This is so important! In all of the things that you do; from meeting someone, to slow dripping them, there is only one goal in mind: to have them trust you enough to give you a chance to show them what you could do for them given the opportunity to do so. In as much as they must trust you, they also must think of you when they next have need for your service of product.

When a 'Money in Motion' event happens, it can have an energy and momentum all of its' own. If you haven't had contact with this person for some time, they might not think of you once they are caught up in the circumstances that have caused 'Money to go in Motion'. Perhaps they have received an inheritance. If this is the case then someone they were close to has died. Perhaps they have received a severance package as part of being let go. Events such as these can be very emotional. However, it could be a positive event such as a raise or bonus, a new job, or even winning the lottery. Whatever their emotional state, if not contacted on a regular basis, they may not think of you when they need you the most!

In addition to trusting you, there must be enough contact and familiarity so that the person either automatically thinks of you when they have a need for your product or service, or you are right there for them when the event occurs.

Positioning yourself properly is why ongoing contact in one form or another needs to be maintained. You want to be right there when the need arises, and you want to know that given this opportunity, this person will become your customer.

3. Landing a New Customer When 'Money goes in Motion'—Having a presentation that lands them every time.

Yes, people must trust you to think of you as a serious candidate for their business. Yes, people must think of you when they have a need for your service. The end of the relationship curve, for better or for worse, comes when you show them what you do, how you do it and how you can help them. At the end of your presentation, you will either have landed a new customer or not. If you have, then a new relationship will begin. That of a customer, which is always different from what it was before they took this last step and trusted you to deliver to them what you promised. This trust changes all future interactions. Now they do return your calls. Now they do pay attention when you talk to them about a new product. Customers want to hear what you have to say that will improve their circumstance.

I also found that if my presentation was not good enough, most of the time I did not get another opportunity. If your presentation is not good enough to land them at this time when they had a need for your product or service, this rejection will act as a huge impediment from their giving you another opportunity in the future. One exception might be if your product simply was not the best solution, you were honest and forthright in this acknowledgement, and at a later day, due to an upgrade in your product suite or service, you could now offer them something that is exactly right. However, only if they still need whatever you offer.

A major hurdle could be that money will no longer be in motion. Their need has been satisfied for now, a new relationship established, they have no desire to invest the time, or energy needed to make a change they no longer feel is necessary.

As discussed elsewhere, your presentation is your last opportunity on the relationship curve to build trust through prospecting. Whatever opinions they may have accumulated about you over the period they have come to know you, this is your time to shine. They are going to see you at your best and the last piece will fall into place. You will receive your reward for the time, energy, and costs you have incurred bringing this relationship to this last step:

"A new customer has been born!"

CHAPTER 5

BUILDING YOUR PIPELINE

Wouldn't it be great to have a pipeline of prospects who have the potential to be some of your best customers?

Do you have a pipeline? It is amazing how many people don't have a pipeline. Let me show you how to start a pipeline. You will be surprised how many new people you add to this pipeline are people you already know, and with whom you have a level of trust. Discover how to capture new people for your pipeline. As you do, find out how your pipeline will become a growing pool of relationships maturing into continuous presentation opportunities.

Kick Start Checklist

✓ Have you started a pipeline?
✓ How will you get a commitment from people to one day do business with you?
✓ How are you "positioned" with the people in your pipeline?

CHAPTER 5

BUILDING YOUR PIPELINE

Everyone who is in your pipeline is there for one reason: you have determined that they are qualified to one day become your customer. Now that they are there, you can direct all your activities to one goal: to build sufficient familiarity and trust so when they have a need for your product or service, you will be one of the service providers given an opportunity to present your value proposition.

One of the questions I like to ask when giving seminars is, "Do you have a pipeline?" It amazes me how many successful producers do not have a pipeline. The more successful you are, the busier you are managing your existing customer base and handling the new business that comes your way. Unless you are growing at a pace you are happy with (and you would not be attending my seminar or reading this book if you were), you need to have a pipeline. It is the beginning of your new growth process.

A pipeline is simply a database of all your prospects. By channeling them into this pipeline, you enable yourself to move them methodically along the relationship curve until the time when they are ready to become your customer. Having them in your pipeline ensures that you are contacting them frequently enough so that you are positioned for the time when 'Money goes in Motion'. Nothing can be more frustrating than discovering someone you thought you knew very well, but had not spoken to for some time, had acquired your service or product from a competitor. When you ask them why they did not contact you, they apologize and tell you that the other person initiated and drove the process, and they hadn't thought of you. Don't let this happen to you! You must communicate frequently enough with your prospects that they naturally think of you, or you are right there when they have a need for what you have to offer.

Important decisions normally do not happen quickly. Usually someone has been thinking about doing something for some time before they finally take action. You must be sure you have a diary system that causes people in your pipeline to "pop up" and forces you to deal with them—either by contacting them, or making a new diary note at which time they will "pop up" again. Without a well-organized system, you will not contact many of these people regularly. You must have an efficient system: prospects must not be lost; promised letters or materials must be sent; diary notes must not be missed. From the moment you capture someone for your pipeline you must efficiently move them along to the day when they become your customer. Promised materials not being sent, telephone calls or a meeting being forgotten or missed can undermine all you have done to date.

"You Must Be Organized!"

Another great thing about a pipeline is that it enables you to contact everyone in it regularly, and with a minimum of effort. A simply way you can do this is by sending a newsletter or correspondence to your entire pipeline. This way, even if you have not recently called them, they will receive something that keeps you and the services you offer right in front of them. It helps them to get to know you; it helps them to remember you; it creates a level of familiarity so that the next time you call them, you are not a stranger, instead you are the person who has been in touch with them frequently over the years.

Once you have captured someone for your pipeline, the rest is easy if you are organized—follow up and "slow drip automatically happen. No one is missed.

** *See Chapter 18 for further information on "slow drip".*

How do you start a pipeline? Easy. First, think of all the people you know who currently are not your customers, but you would like them to be. If you know them, you probably have already built some level of trust with them. That's great! Put them in your database: their name; address; phone numbers; occupation, etc. What else do you need to know to qualify them as a potential customer? Have you asked them these things? Have you met them? Have you had a face-to-face information gathering meeting so you can do an analysis of their situation to determine whether you can be of service to them at this time? Do you know when they might next have a need for what you have to offer?

"Are you positioned with them?"

Once you have everyone you know who qualifies as a potential customer in your pipeline, it is time to add to this foundation people you do not know, but who qualify as potential customers. People come into your pipeline from all sorts of directions: a list of some sort, a referral, an advertisement or promotion, a meeting or seminar. The more business development activities you have on the go, the more people will end up in your pipeline. The most important thing you can do as you contact people, is to capture them in your database and very methodically follow up and slow drip them until the day they become your customer, or you decide that they are no longer worth following up on. As the years go by your pipeline will grow and grow. So too will the relationships you have with the people who are in you pipeline. As this happens, the most powerful ingredient of all will take place—Life!

That's right—Life. People's lives are constantly changing. Many of the people in your pipeline with whom you have built a level of trust, are going to find themselves in a situation where they have a need and a desire for your service or product. When this happens, they are going to think of you! They will call you because you have been gently reminding them to call since you first contacted them, and somewhere along the way, you asked for a commitment.

"The next time you have a need for what I have to offer, will you give me an opportunity to show you what I can do for you?"

By getting this commitment and staying in touch frequently enough to be aware of changes in their life, when 'Money goes in Motion' for them, you will get an opportunity to do a presentation for them. As discussed later, when this opportunity comes, your presentation will be so good that you will land the customer every time.

A mature pipeline is a very exciting thing. It develops energy of its own. New people going in; existing people contacted and followed up on; 'Money going in Motion' frequently; presentation opportunities are happening and new customers being born on a regular basis.

It all starts with the first person you put in your pipeline. After that, everyone simply flows right in and your systems take over until the day they become a customer.

If you do not have a pipeline, start one! If you do have one, review it. Do you have the information you need to slow drip effectively? Do you have a diary system for appropriate follow up for each individual? Do you have a newsletter? When was the last time you contacted everyone in your pipeline? Did you get a commitment from each one of them to give you an opportunity to present your value proposition when they next have a need for your product or service?

Your customer base is the measurement of your current success.

"Your pipeline is the vehicle that will fuel your future success!"

CHAPTER 6

START WITH THE END IN MIND

Are you ready to go?

If you are reading this book in hopes that you can inject some new energy into your business, you are about to get busy. Learn how a disciplined and focused attack will create a number of presentation opportunities that will result in new customers. However, before you get started, you have to be ready to go. Find out what you must do to be ready for the new prospects and presentation opportunities that are about to happen for you.

Kick Start Checklist

✓ What do you want to accomplish?
✓ How will you follow up?

CHAPTER 6

START WITH THE END IN MIND

If you are ready to inject some serious energy into your business, this book is your template. As you read through it, think about the direction you want this energy to flow. Who are your best customers? What traits do they share? With what type of people do you feel the most comfortable and confident? Where can you find more people like that? Think about networking opportunities. Make sure you direct part of your energy into creating and/or building a networking group of some sort. (See Chapter 20)

"Whom should you call?"

Once you start calling prospects, you need to be efficient in your follow up. You need an introductory letter and package; you should have a form of automatic communication with your entire pipeline—a newsletter perhaps; and you must have a contact management system that will ensure you will capture information, make notes of conversations, and provide for effective and efficient follow up. Do you have these things ready to go?

Dr. Stephen Covey once said, "Start with the end in mind."

The whole purpose of your disciplined and focused attack is to create a number of presentation opportunities that will result in your landing new customers. You are going to introduce yourself to new people; hopefully meet most of them; find out everything you can about them; position yourself, and one day be given an opportunity to present your value proposition. If you do not have a presentation template that will land them when given this opportunity, all your previous work will be for nothing. Usually you do not get a second chance. There is no point in working hard to get these opportunities if you are not ready to capitalize on them.

Therefore, while you are working on building your pipeline, you need to create your value proposition as well as your analysis and presentation template. Read chapter 23 and 24 and get these ready. You could call exactly the right person at exactly the right time, right out of the gate. Let's not lose them if this happens.

OK. Now you are ready. You know whom you want to call, you will follow up efficiently once you capture them for your pipeline, and you're ready to land them when you get the opportunity to do so.

Away you go!

CHAPTER 7

YOU HAVE TO BELIEVE IN THE PROCESS

Have you ever closed your eyes, took a deep breath, and stepped off into the unknown?

How do you stay motivated when you are working extremely hard and don't seem to be getting anywhere? Learn how to focus on measurable results that will translate into business opportunities. Find out how to overcome discouragement with a business model that rewards you for the effort along the way. See the critical mass of your pipeline grow and with it the number of presentation opportunities presented to you. More and more people who have come to trust you are going to have 'Money go in Motion' in their life and are going to give you the opportunity to make them your customer. Be inspired to believe enough, not to give up, to dig deep, and force yourself to continue to make the effort.

Kick Start Checklist

✓ What goals will you set to measure your efforts?
✓ How will you reward yourself?

CHAPTER 7

YOU HAVE TO BELIEVE IN THE PROCESS

Regardless of what business activities you are involved in, one thing is certain:

"You have to believe!"

Previously I mentioned that there are 3 steps to the Sales Process. Once again they are:

STEP 1   Introducing yourself to someone new.

STEP 2   Building a relationship and positioning yourself.

STEP 3   Landing the customer when 'Money goes in Motion'.

The reason it is critical that you believe in the process is that it takes time, and you must not give up before the results begin to show themselves.

Over the course of building three clienteles in the Investment industry, I have discovered that, on average, the number of contacts to land a client was seven, and there was at least one meeting included in this average. It takes time to build a relationship and position yourself for the sale, and it is critical that you do not rush the process. If you do, many times you will burn the relationship and never get the opportunity to make your presentation.

Regardless of the type of business you are in, it will take some time for you to make new introductions, meet these people, and position yourself with them. In time, they will have a need for your product or service and, if you have not rushed the process, they will give you the opportunity to present your value proposition and you will make them your customer.

Once you make a commitment to "The Pipeline", you will be instantly making a great effort, but for at least 3 months, you may only see modest results. However, do not be discouraged. Your pipeline will be growing, and you must believe that the numbers will come through for you in the end. Because at first that is all you have—the numbers. This is your only measurement of success. To believe in your heart that the effort will yield results, and to be prepared to put your head down and work harder when you don't seem to be getting anywhere, I believe, is the secret of success.

You must keep a record of your efforts because early on that's all you have! The results will not come if you do not believe. You must force yourself to keep grinding away and trying to make the numbers happen, even when you do not seem to be getting anywhere. However, as you make the calls and your pipeline grows; as you have the meetings and your relationships grow; as you position yourself and get the opportunities, before you know it you will just be trying to keep up as your momentum kicks in.

Along the way, you have to reward yourself for the effort you are making. In Chapter 11 I will discuss how to use call sheets to help you keep track of your efforts. As you achieve your targets each week, you need to think of a way to reward yourself. What would you like to do? Go to a movie? Play a round of golf? Work hard to achieve your goals and when you do, take the time off and enjoy this success. Acknowledge your accomplishments and know that in achieving this small success week in and week out, you will accomplish the increase in business and the success you are working so hard to achieve.

As your pipeline grows and starts to gain momentum, it then becomes a lot of fun. You are just trying to keep up with it and are making a lot of money for doing so.

CHAPTER 8

YOU HAVE TO BELIEVE IN YOURSELF

How good a job do you do for your customers?

Do you believe in yourself? Do you feel you are the best person with the best solutions for your prospects needs? Find out how to inject conviction and passion into all that you do. Discover how changes in your delivery and demeanor can result in better conversations, meetings that are more productive, and more presentation opportunities.

Kick Start Checklist

✓ Do you inject enthusiasm into all your conversations?
✓ Do you always say what you believe, with a passion and conviction that leaves no doubt?

CHAPTER 8

YOU HAVE TO BELIEVE IN YOURSELF

You must have confidence in yourself if you want others to have confidence in you. You must honestly believe that the product or service that you have to offer will truly add value to this person's life and that you are the person with the right solution to meet this person's needs.

I have always had a simple rule. I will never recommend anything, to anybody, that I do not believe is the right thing for them. By adopting this simple rule, my reputation has grown as the years have gone by. People have come to know and trust that if I am recommending something, it is the right thing for them.

Expressed in all that I do is this conviction. When doing a presentation of my services, I always do so with a desire to do business with this person for the rest of their life, or my career. How will I feel later about this person accepting my advice and following my recommendations? A month from now? Six months from now? One year from now? Will I be able to look them in the eye, no matter what should happen, and know I based my recommendations solely on what I honestly believed was right for them?

You have an obligation in your business to be sure that you base your recommendations on a sound and knowledgeable understanding of the product or service you are providing. You have an obligation to your customers to be current on industry trends and innovations to ensure you are recommending the latest enhancements, or utilizing the best analytical tools that are available to you. This means you will be constantly striving to be the most current, the most knowledgeable, and the best at what you do.

"Do you believe in yourself and what you have to offer?"

Trust is very important. Passion and conviction, when trust is in place, is an incredibly powerful combination. You will find that this combination; trust, passion and conviction will grow into a reputation for honesty and integrity in your profession, and will be a powerful source of new customers and referrals.

If you truly believe in what you have to offer, you should have no problem speaking about it with conviction and passion. I find that when I am passionate about something, I usually get excited when I start talking about it. Knowing that what you have to offer is exactly right for someone, seeing them understanding why, and watching them become as excited as you are is a very gratifying feeling.

However, when I do not truly like something, or if I have any doubts, it is very hard for me to get excited or passionate about it. If you are not excited, it is going to be almost impossible to get the person you are talking to excited about it.

"If you truly believe in what you are offering, become passionate about it!"

You will find your convictions will create an excitement that was not there before, and that will be irresistible to your customers.

CHAPTER 9

THE POWER
OF PROJECTS

Do you know the secret of converting good ideas into action?

Do you have a number of things you would like to do, but cannot seem to get done? How do you convert good ideas into an action plan? Find out how to turn your ideas into projects. Use the project worksheet to define your objectives and to book the needed time into your agenda. Discover how projects can create energy of their own. Learn how to convert this energy into new relationships and business opportunities.

Kick Start Checklist

✓ Have you prioritized all your pending activities?
✓ What projects have you been meaning to do, but have not found the time for?
✓ Have you completed a project worksheet for each activity you would like to finish?
✓ When will you work on these projects?

CHAPTER 9

THE POWER
OF PROJECTS

Do you find that when you undertake a new activity it inspires a burst of energy? I do. I am very project oriented. To focus exclusively on one idea or activity for a set period is very powerful. This time will vary according to what project I am working on. Whether it is as simple as mowing the lawn or cleaning out the garage, I find that once I get going, I find a burst of energy and get it done. It may take me awhile to get around to doing it, but once I do, I get it done.

I apply this same principle to all that I do. Get it done and drive on. If I am going to do it, I might as well attack it with a focused burst of energy and do the great job I know I can do. Because I know this about myself, I undertake many projects. In fact, I treat almost everything I need to do as a project.

The first thing I do is give the task a name. By doing so, I force myself to take something that is conceptual "I should make some new business development calls" and make it real "New Contacts for October". Once I have given it a name, it becomes an item on my "To Do" list. I will now prioritize it, and, because it is now a "project", I will need to determine:

✓ What are the objectives of the project?
✓ What do I need to do to accomplish this objective?
✓ When will I work on this project?
✓ What is my target date to complete?
✓ How will I monitor the results?

Giving a name to a required job, and making it a project, will force you to budget time to work on it. Let me give you an example. Would you like to be very busy for a couple of months? I can show you how in the next 5 minutes, you can start a project that will force you to be very busy for the next two months? Ready? Book a meeting room somewhere for between 50 to 100 people for two months from now. There! That one little thing is now going to keep you very busy for the next two months.

Now, here is what you now need to do:

1) Identify your best clients or customers, or those who have the potential to be.
2) Think of something that they all have in common: music, the arts, health—there are so many topics to choose from.
3) Whatever you choose, you must find a person or perhaps a combination of people, in that profession who would be interested in doing a talk about it.

That is all you need to do to get the event set up. You can build and embellish this in whatever way you can afford. You could tie it into a meal, a social, or a seminar. You could have coffee and pastries, or not. You could pay for the whole event yourself, charge people so you break even on the project, or you could charge them and donate the proceeds to charity. As this event is yours, you have the flexibility to do as you like.

You are about to get very busy. Think of all your current customers, as well as people you would like to have as customers. Phone them all. Let them know you are putting on an event; ask them if they would like to come, and if they know of anyone who would like to come.

You have just made yourself very busy, a good type of busy, for the next while. You are going to have a conversation with each of your best customers, and with a number of potential customers. You will be doing so in a complimentary (they are important enough to be invited), non-threatening (they know you are not going to sell them anything) way. This conversation, and hopefully your visit with them at the event, will help you build on these relationships. It, perhaps, will be an opportunity to meet them for the first time. For some, it will be another step in the path towards getting to know you, like you, and trust you enough to become your customer. For those who are already your customer, it will provide an opportunity to add value to the relationship and to, perhaps, introduce you to their family and friends.

Projects such as the one described above can be of any size. They can be as small as calling a few people for a special reason and taking less than an hour or so big that it might take you a month or more to complete.

As you are creating projects to convert some of your ideas into reality, something else will happen—you will suddenly have a whole bunch of new projects that are demanding your attention. Now what are you going to do? Can you get to all of them? You may not be able to, but by making them all real, now you will be able to prioritize them. Make a list. Write them all down. How important is each one? Is this one more important than this other one? After you have sorted them according to importance, now you need to figure out how to find the time to work on the most important ones. Take a minute to look at every one. How much time do you need to focus on each of them? When is the deadline for completion?

Once you have done this analysis, there is one more step. You will need to allocate time for each of them. To do this, each week I look at the following week and visualize each day: Monday is usually my paperwork day. Which of the important projects require planning and organization? It is a good day to allocate some hours to these important projects. What about Tuesday? Perhaps I plan to be in the office in the morning, and I have some meetings out of the office in the afternoon. Since one of my projects is New Contacts for the month, I am going to allocate one hour Tuesday morning between 8:00 and 9:00 specifically for business development calls. For the afternoon, I am going to try to set up one new meeting for while I am out.

Do the same for each day of the week. Where will you be? What do you need to do? What are your highest priorities? What smaller activities can you schedule between the larger projects that you need to spend time on?

Doug E. Lachance

I find that when I visualize my day, my week, or my month, I can feel whether the activities I have planned are too many, too few, or just enough. Try it. You will be surprised at the results.

The more projects you have on the go the busier you will be. See Appendix 2 (Forms) for a project worksheet to get you going.

CHAPTER 10

YOU MUST BE FOCUSED

Do you think you can block everything out for an hour or two?

Would you like to increase your productivity dramatically? Think what it would do to your results if you were talking to more people; visiting with more people; getting more presentation opportunities. Discover the power of a focused effort. Learn how to do more things in less time, leaving extra time for yourself and all the other things you have to do.

Kick Start Checklist

✓ Can you focus exclusively on one activity for a short time?
✓ How will you measure your progress?

CHAPTER 10

YOU MUST BE FOCUSED

If I could pick the one thing that has contributed most to my success, it is my ability to focus. When I am working on something, I give it 100% energy and attention. I do not let myself become distracted.

Over the years, I have had many opportunities to watch others in action. Many times, I have seen advisors calling on the phone: they make a call; stop; input the information and notes. Something on their desk or, someone walking by will distract them, and the next thing you know 10 or 15 minutes will have gone by before they make the next call.

When the time comes for me to focus on making calls, I do it much differently. While I am making calls, I use 5 x 8 cards to make notes of the conversation. As soon as the call has ended, I set the card aside and immediately pick up the phone to make another call. For the next hour or two (whatever time I have allotted) I will not be distracted. If someone interrupts me (unless it is an emergency), I will tell him or her that I will get back to him or her at a certain time (depending on my schedule). At the end of the day, I give all my cards to my assistant to input into the databank, and for delivery of any letters or materials that I have made note of on the cards.

"I do not get distracted!"

As a result, when I am calling, I am extremely productive. Call after call, non-stop for an hour or two at a time, yields incredible results.

I do the exact same with non-calling activities. If I am planning a seminar, or organizing a mailing or promotional strategy, when it comes time to work on the project, I work on it and nothing else. You will be amazed at how much more productive you are when you commit 100% of your focus and energy to one thing at a time.

"Do not let yourself be distracted!"

Allocate specific amounts of time to an activity. When the scheduled time comes, blank everything else out and focus. How many people could you speak to in an hour if you focused on calling, and really tried to speak to as many as you could? Try it for a few hours. Have fun with it! Can you beat that number next time? See what your best is. You will be amazed how much you can do when you really try hard.

"Focus!"

CHAPTER 11

THE MOST IMPORTANT PRINCIPLE

Do you want it bad enough?

If you want it, learn how to make it happen. Learn to force yourself to make the numbers happen, and reward yourself when you do. Learn how to set achievable goals and reach them. Discover the power that Call Sheets can have on your productivity. Use them to motivate you to work harder, especially at those times when it is toughest to do so. Find out how to end each week with positive results.

Kick Start Checklist

✓ Do you know how to use a call sheet?
✓ How will you increase your cold and warm calling results every week?

CHAPTER 11

THE MOST IMPORTANT PRINCIPLE

"You have to make the contacts!"

Many of you will not make it past this Principle. This one thing causes most people to wash out. It cannot be broken. All success flows from it.

The numbers create an energy and momentum. Imagine a pond. You reach down, pick up a rock, and throw it. It makes a splash and small ripples flow outward from the momentum of the impact. Now imagine you pick up a boulder and throw it. The ripples are now waves and on and on they go.

This is what you need to do. Make a great effort. Throw a boulder; create waves; and the energy and momentum will follow. As the years go by, your pipeline will grow and mature. The rewards for this effort and energy will be in the many presentation opportunities that occur as your relationships grow and 'Money goes in Motion'. One day, your prospects will have the need, the ability and desire to buy, and the trust in you to deliver, that will make them a new customer.

It does not matter what way you prefer to contact people. The key is:

"You must make personal contact!"

Relationships cannot grow without personal contact. Without growing relationships, trust cannot grow and, without trust, strangers cannot make the transition to become customers.

"You must do the numbers!"

The target is 20 contacts on average per day—100 per week. These must be personal contacts. Leaving messages or talking to secretaries does not count. You must have talked directly to the person you were trying to reach.

For the most part, this personal contact will be a simple telephone call. This is the most time effective method of contact. If you do not like to talk on the phone, it is a lot harder to make the numbers happen, and they must happen! If you do enjoy talking to people, the numbers can be extremely rewarding; you will reach a point where you are paid handsomely to simply meet with your customers, both old and new.

The most valuable contact happens anytime you have a one on one, face-to-face meeting. Telephone calls are an excellent tool for keeping in touch or delivering information, but it is in a face-to-face meeting that a relationship grows, you gain trust, and information is gathered. This is the first and most important step in positioning yourself.

If you presently have a customer base, your business calls with those customers will count towards your numbers. Service conversations with customers—discussing administration issues (i.e. statements, check requests, etc) do not count. It must be a call that could generate business with this customer (i.e. reviews, calling to discuss a new product, etc).

The total per day must be 20. You must fill in the gap between your current customer calls that generate an income and the 100 per week average with potential new customers. Start to build a pipeline of potential customers. Stay in touch with them in an organized way. Use the time you are able to spare from productively managing your exiting book of business.

You should target everything in your business plan towards making meetings happen. Whether a meeting is for coffee or drinks, lunch or dinner, a seminar, an appointment at their office (or home) or yours, or even in a social setting, the more face-to-face interactions you have with the people in your pipeline, the more dramatic your success will be. One day, all your time will be spent in presentations and reviews; and your team will make the meetings happen, and handle customer service and administration.

Face-to-face meetings or visits take more time and are more valuable. In my system, they are worth 3 telephone contacts. Your target should be at least 8 visits per week and that would count as 24 towards your total contact number of 100. Seminars or group meetings are a great way of making contacts, and they can help you hit your target for the week quickly. Any combination will do. You will also be able to relax and enjoy taking an afternoon off if you know you have hit the numbers that week. Often, I would really focus early in the week and then reward myself on Thursday or Friday with a golf game.

"However, you must hit your goal of 100 per week!"

The numbers are magical. In building all three of my clienteles, I always maintained the consistency in the numbers. I tried to be solidly over the minimum, and I kept track to be sure that I was. (I decided that if an average of 20 per day would do it, my goal would be 23 or 24 just to make sure!)

The more contacts ultimately translate to more customers. The bigger the pipeline, the greater the number of opportunities, the more new customers, and the higher income or revenue will be from this new business.

It is critical that you have a call sheet. (See Appendix 2 for samples) You must keep track of your calls or you will not achieve your target. Call sheets force you to dig deep and make a few more calls when you really do not want to. For every clientele I have built, I have used call sheets in the early years.

"You must make the contacts! You cannot succeed if you do not!"

It is not only in the early years that I have used call sheets. Over the years, anytime I felt that my effort was lagging, I would bring out the call sheets. Sure enough, I would discover that I was not hitting the 100 calls per week average. By using the call sheets once again, it would force me to put in the same effort that caused me to be successful in the first place.

If you are successful at what you do, you may believe that cold calling is an unproductive use of your time. You are busy trying to make a living.

You only want to talk to people who are interested in what you do and have to offer.

Get someone to cold call for you! Perhaps hire a student to cold call for you. I have found students in business courses to be excellent cold callers. Let someone else do the initial cull so the calls you are making are already warm.

However, you must still hit your personal target of 100 per week.

Your calls will now be more productive because the people you are talking to are qualified for whatever it is you have to offer. As you are busy hitting your target of 100 calls per week, many of these calls will be building relationships with people who will one day be your customer.

No matter where you are in the success curve, try using call sheets for a while. You will be amazed at how your productivity will improve.

The Roller Coaster

Selling is a lot like riding a roller coaster. Some days are an incredible high, and some days an unbelievable low.

There is no greater feeling than landing a big customer. Days when you have a great breakthrough are an incredible high. Days when you have grinded away through 18 or 19 calls that have not gone well can be an incredible low. Can this many people not like you?

There will be times when you just cannot force yourself to talk to anybody at all. This happens. Distract yourself. Work on your paperwork for a day. Tackle some project that has been on the backburner. Alternatively, just get out of the office.

Sometimes you need to get away. Take an afternoon off. Go see a movie. Do not be afraid to take a break. Just make sure you have earned it. Hit your contact goal of 100 for the week. Force yourself. If you do end up short one week, make it up the next.

I believe when you are working, you should work hard. If you are not going to work hard, you should not be there. Get away for a while. When you come back, be ready to really focus and work hard again.

CHAPTER 12

HOW TO GET YOUR BEST CUSTOMERS TO REFER THEIR FAMILY AND FRIENDS TO YOU

How would you like to be meeting people who already know you, trust you, and are ready to do business with you?

Learn how to make your best customers want to refer new customers to you. Let me show you how to create customer advocates who are constantly telling everyone about you. Let me show you strategies that will motivate and act as a catalyst for your best customers to prospect for you.

Kick Start Checklist

✓ What are you doing to create customer "advocates"?
✓ How will you market into your customer base?
✓ Where can you find more people just like your best customers?

CHAPTER 12

HOW TO GET YOUR BEST CUSTOMERS TO REFER THEIR FAMILY AND FRIENDS TO YOU

I cannot emphasize enough how your existing customers are absolutely the best place to start your new business development activities. Do you have all of their business? You could probably double your income or revenues, if you had all of your existing customers business. Have you presented them with a Value Proposition that requires that you have all of their business to do the best possible job?

I have usually managed all of the holdings for most of my clients. The exception was the occasional, very big client who wanted to spread their millions around. Other than these few exceptions, I usually had all the money. The reason for this was that my analysis of their situation always encompassed all of their assets. I told them this was very important. The strategy for the money I was going to manage had to fit with their overall picture.

For those who would not share this information with me, I performed my analysis as if I had all their money and explained conceptually how new money would fit with the strategy. Often, the rest of the money would follow later.

In the investment business, an analysis of a persons' situation is an integral part of the investment process. If you are in a business where an analysis is part of the service you provide, you should do an analysis for all of your best customers to be sure you are up to date on their current situation and to remind them of the reasons why they have chosen you to take care of their needs. Afterwards you should ask them:

"Do you have someone you know who would appreciate me doing this exercise for them? It would act as a great confirmation of whether they are on track. For others, who need help, it can act as an excellent roadmap."

Regardless of what industry you are in, you should try to create an analysis template that will give you an opportunity to showcase your value proposition. By doing so, you will create an opportunity to add value for someone by simply showing them the products and services you have available. In addition to discovering needs you perhaps were not aware of, this will also open the door for you to ask them if they know someone who may benefit from what you have to offer.

The most successful business people know that strong customer relationships are the key to growing your business. To keep your customers, and give them the confidence to refer new business to you, you need to earn and cultivate their loyalty.

To boost your business exponentially, you need to have ecstatic customers who will become your advocates. Customer advocates do business with you exclusively and repeatedly go out of their way to refer new business to you. Obviously, you must provide great service to create customers advocates. It is not enough to do a great job however. You must think of ways to inspire and motivate them to give referrals for you to their family and friends. Make your customers feel they are an integral part of your business.

Have you heard of the Rule of 52? This rule states that each of your best customers has an inner circle of approximately 52 close friends, family members, and business associates. These inner circles constitute your best group of potential prospects

Here are some ideas to help you motivate your customers to introduce their "inner circle" to you!

A. CUSTOMER ADVISORY COUNCIL

A Customer Advisory Council is one of the most powerful ways to create customer advocates. By making your best customers part of a forum to:

- provide feedback about your current service;
- test and provide input on initiatives you are considering;
- share their best ideas with you;

they will feel they have helped to make you as good as you are. They will want to tell their friends and family about you because they were influential in the process and they feel they are part of the service you are providing. As active participants, your most valued customers will become closer to your business.

As valuable as the actual results of the process are, it is the customer relationship perspective given by your customer advisory council that is powerful. They will tell you what they like about your service and what they do not. They will bring deficiencies to your attention, so you can correct them, before customers leave without telling you why. When you are planning to launch a new initiative, you can test it first to be sure you do not put a lot of dollars, time, or energy into something that is not going to get the results you anticipated. Perhaps they will fine-tune it for you. One of the most exciting benefits will be the great ideas that come from the group. When your best customers start brainstorming with you, and for you, you can be sure that good ideas will follow.

You have great flexibility in choosing the venue for your council. These are your best customers. Either you may host the get together as a very professional affair in your boardroom, or you may decide to pamper them and take them out to a nice dinner.

Choose your best team. Select 8 to 12 of your most valued customers. Consider those:

- whose business, judgment, and opinions you value greatly.
- whom you would like to keep forever and replicate.
- who will offer their opinions.

Two Caveats:

1. Do not invite an unhappy customer regardless of size. You do not want this person to poison the others. Take this customer out one on one to find out what you can do to make them happy.

2. If it is your best customers, do not invite someone who does not qualify. It may undermine the whole process with some of the other attendees.

B. FOCUS GROUP

A focus group is similar to a Customer Advisory Council in that you bring customers together. With a focus group however, you invite customers who share characteristics or interest. You can target certain niches within your business. These groups could be professionals, empty nesters, retirees, or business owners. The list is almost endless. Focus on the groups that seem to be full of your best customers.

What are some of the characteristics shared by a certain group of your customers? You likely will not be able to approach retirees with the same message as a young professional. Find a group that will share a common interest. Get them together. They will enjoy the meeting and talking to each other. They will feel like valued customers. The, will want to invite their friends, who share the same interests, to become part of it.

Your primary goals with each group will be to bring them together and learn from them. They will appreciate the opportunity to network with each other, and they will provide you with feedback and insight about your service.

C. RESOURCE NETWORK

Depending on your business, you may be in the unique position to offer your customers an opportunity to participate in your network. If you have customers from a variety of industries and services, you can easily build a resource network from within your customers with different backgrounds.

To create an advocate, you must add value to the relationship. One of the best ways to add value is to be able to solve problems. Creating a resource network will do that. Customers will appreciate this service because sometimes it is extremely hard to find good people for specific needs they might have.

In addition to the goodwill you will receive from providing this service, you will also be making the customers that are within your network very happy. You are sending them new customers. They will appreciate the business and they, in turn, will want to refer their customers to you.

There are two ways to build your Resource Network:

1. Look into your customer base. Make a list of all their professions and businesses.

2. Ask your customers to help you identify candidates that would qualify for your network.

Once you have compiled a complete list, if there is more than one candidate, you will have to choose your supplier for that category. Be certain those who you do choose will do a good job, and will stand behind their work. Your customers will blame you if instead of solving a problem you create a new one. Do your due diligence!

D. CUSTOMER SURVEY

When designed and used properly, surveys can provide valuable information that will supplement your regular customer meetings and phone conversations. An effective survey can help you identify unhappy customers, pinpoint product and service items that need improvement, and help generate referrals.

Encouraging active customer participation in your business increases your customer loyalty—they will feel they have invested time and thought into helping you build and improve your business.

Build a Customer Survey

There are 4 steps involved in executing this project:

1. Send a Letter
   - Have an incentive (hockey tickets, donation etc)
   - Have self addressed, postage paid return envelopes
   - Have a deadline for replies (2 weeks recommended)

   (For a Sample Letter, see Appendix 2: Forms.)

2. Evaluation Form

   Include your Evaluation Form

   (For a sample Evaluation Form, see Appendix 2: Forms)

3. Follow Up

   Follow up directly with all those who participated in the survey. Send a letter or thank you note to them. Consider sending a letter to your customer base sharing with them the results of the survey. They will be familiar with the questions, having received the survey, and will be interested in how others felt.

   (For a sample Follow up Letter, see Appendix 2: Forms)

4. Referrals

   The "P.S." has proven to be one of the most powerful parts of a letter. Many times people will read the P.S. before the letter itself. You should always be looking for referral opportunities and your survey is a great time to do so. Here are examples of some you can try:

   P.S. Some of my customers have recently asked me if I accept referrals. I would certainly appreciate the opportunity to be of service to any family members or business associates that you might refer.

   P.S. If you are speaking to someone who is looking for a second opinion, I would be pleased to contact him or her. I will work hard to ensure the person you refer feels that it is a wise investment of time.

P.S. I would like to thank my clients for introducing their friends and family members to me throughout the year. As you know, I have built my business on word of mouth advertising and it is a great compliment to receive a referral.

P.S. As you can imagine, a business like mine thrives on word of mouth advertising. The most sincere form of compliment I can receive is a referral from one of my valued clients.

P.S. We recently developed a _____, and a number of customers have requested one for their parents or a close friend. If you know someone who needs _____, I would be pleased to send him or her one.

P.S. I thank all my customers who have referred their friends and family members to me. I appreciate your confidence in my abilities. If you know of others interested in the services I provide, please have them call me at _____.

"Remember to always thank your customers for a referral. Send a 'Thank You' note regardless of whether the person becomes a customer or not!"

CHAPTER 13

FINDING MORE PEOPLE JUST LIKE YOUR BEST CUSTOMERS

How can you find more people just like your best customers?

Discover how to find more people just like your best customers. Where are they? What sources and strategies are available to find them? What characteristics do all of your best customers share? What is their age? Their income? Where do they live? Where do they work? Where are more people just like them?

Kick Start Checklist

✓ What traits do your ideal customers share?
✓ How will you find more people just like your best customers?

CHAPTER 13

FINDING MORE PEOPLE JUST LIKE YOUR BEST CUSTOMERS

A. DEFINING YOUR IDEAL CUSTOMER PROFILE

Before you start prospecting, you need to know what you are looking for. Wouldn't you like to have more customers just like your best customers? If you do, you need to discover what these best customers have in common. What qualities do they share that qualify them as your best customers?

1. What are your ideal customer profile traits?
   - Age
   - Income
   - Net Worth
   - Occupation
   - Gender
   - Education
   - Residence
   - Family

2. What do your best customers have in common?
   - Why are they your best customers?
   - What types of products or service do they utilize?
   - What is their background?

- What are their hobbies? Social involvements?
- What is your relationship with them?

"Most importantly, how did they become your customer?"

Reviewing how your best customers became customers can provide valuable insight into what works best for you!

B. REVIEW YOUR EXISTING PIPELINE

Arrange to meet and do an analysis for your existing best customers. As you are doing this, you should also be trying to do an analysis for the others in your existing pipeline. Have you qualified everyone? Have you met them? Do you have all the information you require to have to do an analysis for them? Your goal will be the same for your existing pipeline, as for the new people you will be contacting - to position yourself for when 'Money goes in Motion'. Are you positioned with these people?

C. IDENTIFYING POTENTIAL NEW CUSTOMERS

You have defined your ideal customer. You have reviewed your existing pipeline to be sure you have done all you can to qualify, meet and position yourself with everyone in it. Now, you need to find some new people. The better the list, obviously the better the results will be. Although it is all numbers, you can improve your productivity and results by having a better contact list.

Using a phone book, you will be phoning many people who do not have a need for your product or service, and never will. Finding a contact list exclusively of the type of people who would be your best customers is ideal. Use your imagination. Think about what the commonalties your best potential customers would have with each other. With what kinds of people would you like to do business? What characteristics do your best customers share?

The library used to be a great source for lists. Today, the Internet has opened up possibilities that never existed before. Think of your target groups—Doctors, Lawyers, Accountants, Business People, Consultants and/or Tech's—and, either find a membership list, or something that these people or groups have in common.

Quite often, a geographic list can work very well. As one example, many times business owners may cluster together in the industrial sections of a city. There are many small industrial parks. Find them. Obtain a list of all companies, and the key people in these companies, and you have the beginnings of a great list. Where do your best customers work? Are there others just like them close by?

Buying a list is something you may consider. Do you know of a company that provides lists of the demographic profile best suited to your product or service? In the investment business, we use a company in New York that provides a list (by postal code), at a very modest cost, a list of individuals over 50 years old and with incomes over $75,000. They can also provide a list of companies either by revenue or by number of employees. Think about the possibility of buying a list.

Newspapers and magazines can be another great source for lists. Business publications, in particular, are great. Some of the best introductory calls I have had, and ultimately some of my best clients, have come from noticing an award or recognition of some sort. One of the warmest introductory calls is:

"Hello Mr._____. This is Doug Lachance of _____
_____. I wanted to call and congratulate you on _____
_____.

This naturally leads to a discussion of the award or recognition and moves the conversation comfortably to other things. At the end of the call, I would say:
"Well, congratulations once again on _____. I was wondering if it might be okay to send you an introductory letter and my business card?"

This is a very warm call and it is unusual for the person to decline. In the future, the natural reaction to your name will be a positive one due to the warm nature of your first contact.

The Dream 50

If I were to build another clientele, the one thing that I would do for sure, is to think of my Dream 50. This would be the top 50 people that I could imagine having as a client. Being in the investment business, I might choose the CEO of the biggest companies in my area.

A lot of rejection is something I would prepare for. That is OK. Forty-nine rejections would be OK if I landed just one client. And if I don't, if I have made 50 calls, what is one more. Maybe I would make a second Dream 50 since I successfully made it through the first one!

"Get quality names in your pipeline,
and quality customers will come out the other end."

CHAPTER 14

CENTERS OF INFLUENCE

Would you like other people involved in 'Money in Motion' events to refer new business and customers to you?

Let me show you the power of leverage. Centers of Influence are people who are involved with clients during 'Money in Motion' events. Who are the people that your best customers, and people just like them, work with? Who are the people involved in your business's 'Money in Motion' events? How should you introduce yourself to them? Let me show you how to get Centers of Influence to refer their clients and customers to you.

Kick Start Checklist

✓ Who are the 52 people who most want you to succeed?
✓ Who are the people involved in 'Money in Motion' events in your business?

CHAPTER 14

CENTERS OF INFLUENCE

In Chapter 1, I discussed life events that cause 'Money in Motion' events to happen, and cause someone to decide to do, or purchase, whatever it is you have to offer. This entire book is devoted to helping you to find people just like your best customers, and show you how to patiently position yourself with them, and wait for the time that they will give you an opportunity to make them a new customer.

"Wouldn't it be wonderful if, instead of having to find potential customers and wait for a 'Money in Motion' event, people that they trusted referred them to you during these events?"

When this happens, if you have a good "Landing the Customer" template, they should become your customer time after time.

This is a great example of leverage. There is no better form of leverage than cultivating Centers of Influence "advocates" who send you a continuous stream of new business and customers. Absolutely everyone should be patiently, and gently, building a pipeline of these influential business builders.

Before you can begin to cultivate this group, you must figure out who they are. There are two separate types of Centers of Influence. They are:

PERSONAL

Do you remember the Rule of 52 I mentioned? How they say that everyone has a circle of 52 close friends and family around them. What about the 52 close family and friends around you? The family members you are closest to; your best friends; alumni; sports; hobbies; activities. Who are the people in your circle? Write down each of the following:

- Family: Spouse, Parent, Child, Sibling
- Friends
- Clubs
- Church
- Charity
- Hobbies
- Sports
- Activities

Who are the people you know best in each category? Do they all know what you do? Or, how you do what you do? Have you ever shown them your presentation template? Do they know anyone who might need your product or service? Do they know what the 'Money in Motion' events are in your business? Are they on the lookout for these events for you?

"Your friends want you to succeed. Help them to help you do so!"

There is one other type of Center of Influence in the personal category. These are people you know, (or are going to get to know!) who do business with people that that have the potential to be your best customers. Although you will not have the same level of trust as you would from your advocates, this can be a great source of qualified new people for your pipeline. Then, your process will kick in and you will begin to position yourself for the 'Money in Motion' event that will make them your customer.

Some examples of this type of personal Centers of Influence might be:

- Art Dealers
- High End Travel Agents
- Auto Sales Associates
- Jewelers

Once again, who is in this group will depend on your product or service and 'Money in Motion' event.

Who are the people that do business with your best customers? There is a very good chance that they have other customers that you would like to have. Meet them. Get to know them. Perhaps you can refer your customers back and forth to one other.

"Let your best customers tell you where to find more people just like them! Get to know the people with whom they do business."

PROFESSIONALS

The most powerful type of Center of Influence is the professional advisor involved in a 'Money in Motion' event. The clients trust these advisors. Many times, they are relying on them to bring about the successful conclusion of a 'Money in Motion' event. Who are the professionals involved in your 'Money in Motion' events?

Some examples of professionals involved in many 'Money in Motion' events are:

- Accountants
- Lawyers
- Insurance Specialists
- Investment and Financial Advisors
- Bankers
- Real Estate Agents and Specialists
- Company CFO's

"Who are the professionals who are involved in your 'Money in Motion' events?"

HOW DO YOU PROSPECT CENTERS OF INFLUENCE?

You should manage your pipeline of Centers of Influences separately, and handle them differently, than that of your regular pipeline. These people deserve, and must receive special attention.

To begin, I recommend you send an introductory letter, than follow up with a phone call. Be careful here. Do not do too many at a time. You do not want to drop the ball by sending so many letters you are unable to follow up efficiently. Just like a prospect, but with worse consequences, if you blow it with a Center of Influence you will not get a second chance.

"Be professional about everything you do with these people!"

The goal of a follow-up call is to get a meeting, and to show them what you do—a mini presentation. The call might go something like this:

"Hello Mr. Jones? This is Doug Lachance from _____
__. I sent you a letter of introduction recently. Did you receive it?
Great."

"I was hoping that we might get together sometime so I can show
you what I do. There could be a time in the future when we have a
mutual client and I'm hoping that you'll feel very comfortable with
me once you've seen how I do business."

After this, the slow drip is similar to your regular pipeline, but specifically targeted at this group.

One great example of this is something I used to do for Accountants at tax time. I would go to a well-known coffee shop, buy a coffee cup and small bag of ground specialty coffee, and then drop it off with a handwritten note that said:

Hi John!

I know how busy you must be and I thought this might
help.

Best Regards,

Doug

I had a great response from this. Use your imagination. These people are worth it. Small gifts, seminars, events, networking—use every weapon in your arsenal.

"Build a relationship of trust with Centers of Influence and they will build your business for you!"

CHAPTER 15

INTRODUCING YOURSELF

Would you like to introduce yourself to some new people who have the potential to be one of your best customers?

Do you hate cold calling? Most people do. Learn how to overcome this obstacle. Learn how to introduce yourself to new people in a new way. Find out how to make your largest prospects relax, and be willing to talk to you about their situation, and invite you to send them a letter of introduction. Discover the excitement of introducing yourself to people just like your best customers, and capturing them in your ever-growing pipeline, moving towards the day that they will become one of your best customers.

Kick Start Checklist

✓ How will you introduce yourself to new people?
✓ Have you prepared an introductory script to suit both your product, or service, and you?
✓ Will someone cold call for you?

CHAPTER 15

INTRODUCING YOURSELF

A. THE GOAL

The key to the Introductory Call is to introduce yourself to someone and qualify him or her for your pipeline. You have no idea what direction, or with what momentum the relationship will develop. You simply Identify, Qualify, and Capture the Person.

I will talk later about the process and slow drip that begins after the Introductory Call. The most important thing is that you capture them, and very methodically work your way towards being properly positioned for when 'Money goes in Motion'.

B. HOW TO INTRODUCE YOURSELF TO NEW PEOPLE

There are many ways to introduce yourself to someone for the first time, and I will share some ideas with you shortly. First, it is important to understand that once you have identified someone, at some point, you must call him or her to introduce yourself. If you like cold calling, or, if you've decided to hire someone to cold call for you, the scripts in the following sections simply need to be executed by you. If you hate cold calling, here are some ideas that you might try:

    1. Direct Mail—As discussed previously, you may purchase a list of qualified people. Alternatively, you may want to use a geographic list, or some other list comprised of they type of people who have the potential to be your best customers. Send each of them a letter of introduction that includes an invitation to come to an upcoming event you are hosting. (Dinner, seminar, networking group, special event)

2. **Advertising**—Your available budget will determine your advertising initiatives. When you are advertising, the goal is to make new contacts. You must have a reason that will make people want to respond to your ad. This could be a request for information, or an invitation to an event you are hosting.

3. **Radio and TV**—I have hosted a number of shows on Community Cable. In addition to great visibility and credibility, I always tried to give people a reason to contact me on every program. I know of others who have used radio very effectively as well. If you are suited to it and have the opportunity to do so, a radio or TV show is an excellent way to reach out to new people.

As you reach out to connect with people that have the potential to be your best customer, remember that at some point, you will need to introduce yourself personally to them. When that time come, the following process should be followed to capture them for your pipeline.

C. HOW TO MAKE THE INTRODUCTORY CALL

The purpose of the Introductory Call should simply be to qualify the person, and get their approval for entry into your pipeline. This is what else is happening - by agreeing to have you send them an introductory letter, they are unknowingly giving you permission to follow up at sometime in the future. From that point on your system will kick in. Maybe in a few months, maybe over several years, this relationship will continue to grow. This stranger will become a person, then acquaintance, they will gain trust in you, and someday, will have a need and want to become your customer.

In the investment industry, a First Call might go something like this:

"Hello Mr. Smith, my name is _____ and I'm an Investment Advisor at _____. I specialize in _____ _____."

This is where you make a statement that will qualify the prospect, for example...

"My expertise is in helping business owners who control over $1 million in assets find solutions to estate, tax, and investment problems. Are you familiar with __(company name)__?"

If No, the answer would be:

"Oh? We are the oldest and one of the largest full service firms in Canada. Are you an Investor?"

If the answer were Yes, you would say:

"Great. Then you know we are the oldest and one of the largest full service firms in Canada. Are you an Investor?"

If the answer to "Are you an Investor?" is No, you might say:

"Oh? Are you saying that you're not an investor or that you don't have at least $1 million in assets?" (Or whatever your qualifier was.)

If Yes, you would say:

"Great! Are you saying that you are an investor or that you have $1 million in assets?" (Or whatever your qualifier was.)

If they say they are not interested, ask them if that might ever change. Explain to them that, if they qualify, you would like to send them a letter of introduction and your business card so that "Some day down the road, if you ever do have a need for my services, you'll know who I am".

Hopefully, the person will tell you a little something about their situation. You need to know if this person is suitable, and whether they qualify to be your customer at some future time. To do this, you must get them talking about their situation. You have only one goal in your first contact. Is this person worth calling again?

"Are they worth it?"

That is the total purpose of this call, to qualify this person. You are going to put a lot of effort into making this person your customer.

If they do qualify but are not interested at this time, I would follow up and continue to try to meet them. I always try to show in all I do, that a long-term relationship is what is most important to me. If they are not ready to consider me seriously at this time, I will then put them in the pipeline under the category "Long-term Prospect". Although they are currently happy, or do not have a need today, might they in one month, six months, one-year? As you slow drip these people, over the years a familiarity will grow. On that first call, the only question you should have in mind is "Does this person have the potential to one day be your customer". If so, they should be in your pipeline. Your system will then kick in. This modest beginning will automatically start you on the road to a long-term relationship.

When I was building a book of clients, anytime I knew the person had over $1 million dollars in financial assets, I rarely gave up. I would never stop the slow drip.

What is your qualifier? What quality does your current clientele share that could be used to qualify someone new? Is it income? Net worth? Occupation? Family situation? Age? Be definitive. Do not be afraid to ask the right questions. You want everyone in your pipeline to have the potential to be your best customer.

The first call to them becomes an introduction and the beginning to a new process. Perhaps you have already qualified them and know that they would be a great customer. Rarely will someone refuse to let you send him or her an introductory letter. They think that they are getting rid of you, when in fact they are opening the door for you to contact them again. From this point forward, the pipeline kicks in and follow up and slow drip automatically takes place.

Most people like being prospected. It is a compliment. It means they have money, that they are successful. They will be proud of this. Push those buttons.

D. WHAT IF THEY ARE HAPPY WITH THEIR PRESENT SERVICE PROVIDER?

I believe it is critical that if you have found someone you would like to have as a customer someday, you try to get him or her into your pipeline. Following up, and trying to meet with them, will clarify who is truly happy. Many people have an instant shut off switch that clicks in whenever someone phones to prospect them. They do not like being sold anything, they are hit on all the time, and they are automatically very defensive.

> *"You must breakthrough to the other side*
> *of this defense mechanism."*

If they already have a relationship in place for their business, I might say:

> *"I understand that you're happy now, and I respect that. However, is it possible somewhere down the road, you might have a need for someone new? Your existing provider may retire or leave the business. I believe in long-term relationships, and I am hoping that as time goes by, we might get to know each other better. Life has many twists and turns. Perhaps someday in the future you might have a need for my services. Do you mind if I stay in touch?"*

They may still not want to meet you initially. Be sure you have given a good effort to get a meeting and have called them every 2 to 3 weeks for a few months. Then you should continue to slow drip them over the years, with a contact of some sort, every 3 to 6 months.

Other times, they will meet you. From this meeting, you will gain a familiarity and understanding about their personality and situation. This will help you to selectively target their wants and needs, and not just blindly throw various products or ideas at them, hoping that like a fish, they will take the bait sooner or later.

Even if they tell you that they are happy, try to get the meeting before you give up! For those who will not agree to meet you, you must use your imagination. Networking, seminars, and social gatherings are great ways to meet someone. I have found that once you have met someone face-to-face, often they will candidly tell you about their present situation. They might not be as happy as they think!

E. COLD CALLING

I need to talk about this a little bit. Most people I know HATE cold calling.

It is not necessary that you personally cold call. If you are a newcomer at what you do, you probably should do it yourself. It is a good learning experience and prepares you for the important calls you will be making later.

It is great if you are more experienced and like to cold call, but you do not personally have to. It is even better if you can spend 100% of your time on warm calls, talking only to people who are interested in talking to you. Where the rejection and qualification issues have already been eliminated.

However, someone has to make the first call. Prospects have to be gathered and qualified. Someone has to go find them, call them, and qualify them so they can be added to your pipeline. Someone on the team must cold call!

"New people must go into your pipeline
for your customer base to grow!"

One of the difficulties as you become more seasoned is you have less time to devote to prospecting. It is very efficient to hire someone to cold call for you, eliminating 60% to 80% of the time it would otherwise take you. Hire someone and have him or her make the calls and help build your pipeline.

I have found great success with hiring students, who are enrolled in business programs, to call for me. Many of these students are smart, eager, hungry, and energized. For them, it is incredibly exciting to be working for an Advisor in the investment industry.

If you do not like making the calls:

"Hire someone to make the calls for you!"

Moreover, by giving the caller a script and questionnaire, they can do a significant amount of the legwork for you. This will ensure that all the calls you make are warm calls, to people that are ready to talk, and hopefully, meet you.

All the principles and processes outlined in the previous sections of this book remain the same, but the beginning of the conversation starts differently. I might have my hired caller say something like this:

> *"Hello Mr./Mrs. Jones. My name is _____ and I am calling on behalf of Doug Lachance, an Investment Advisor with _____ _____. Doug specializes in _____ (This is where you insert a statement that will qualify the prospect.) and was hoping he could send you an introductory letter, and perhaps be of some service to you at some time point in the future? Are you familiar with _____ "*

If No, the answer would be:

> *"Oh? We are the oldest and one of the largest full service firms in Canada. Are you an Investor"*

If the answer were Yes, they would say:

> *"Great. Then you know we are the oldest and one of the largest full service firms in Canada. Are you an Investor?"*

If the answer to "Are you an Investor" is No, they might say:

> *"Oh? Are you saying that you're not an investor or that you don't have at least $1 million in assets?"* (Or whatever your qualifier was.)

If Yes, they would say:

> *"Great! Are you saying that you are an investor or that you have $1 million in assets?"* (Or whatever your qualifier was.)

Once again, if they say they do not qualify, have your caller ask them if they can see their situation changing. If they say they are not interested, have your caller ask them if that might ever change. Keep track of those who think it might. As with a personal contact, after this call your system will kick in.

Your caller can also use this process for follow up calls, and for trying to arrange meetings for you.

"Hello Mr. Smith. This is _____. I am calling on behalf of Doug Lachance. I spoke to you _____ (1 week, month, etc) ago. I was wondering if you might be interested in my arranging a meeting with Doug to do a complete review and analysis of your situation. People who do this find it to act as a confirmation that their current strategies are on track. Would this be of interest to you?"

There are many ways you can use callers to help you, but I suggest two guidelines for you:

1. Always create scripts for your callers to use.
2. It is rare that a caller can be as good as you are; therefore try to work on your best prospects yourself.

F. FIRST CONTACT FOLLOW UP

After hanging up the phone, it is critical that you have a system in place, whereby:

1. An Introductory letter and other support material (brochure, newsletter, etc.) is mailed promptly - the following day at the latest.

    (An example of an Introductory Letter is in Appendix 2— Forms)

2. Entered in the database is the name, address, phone number, etc for future contact.

3. To record comments and diarize for follow up, an efficient record keeping method must be used! Most of you will use a contact management system. I have one that my assistant updates for me. I personally use 5" x 8" lined index cards. While I am listening, and speaking, I make notes them. As soon as a call is done, I can set the card aside and instantly make the next

call or take another line. When I am done, I give the cards to my assistant for input. If you do not have an assistant, set your notes aside and update your files at the end of the day. Do not let clerical work slow down your contact momentum.

4. A diary note to call back in exactly 2 weeks should be made. The reason to be exact is that, if they were available at that specific time on that specific day, there is a good chance they are regularly available at that time. (Of course, this is only if a more specific time for follow up hasn't been discussed in the call)

G. THE GAME IS ON

When most people hang up the phone, they will completely forget about you. They have no idea that you have now become a part of their life until, either they become a customer, or you decide to give up on them. Little do they know that there is a good chance you will still be talking to them 1 year and possibly 5 to 10 years from now.

"The Game is On!"

When you ask if you can send them a letter, some will say no or make it clear you are wasting your time. Fortunately, there are few truly rude people. If they are worth it, you could diarize them every 6 months, and treat them as an introductory call each time. You will have to decide, on an individual basis, what to do in this situation

When those calls inevitably do happen, you need to end the conversation and carry on.

H. SCRIPTS

I think it is very useful to use a script. Anytime you are making multiple calls with the same purpose or goal, whether it is making a first contact or any other prospecting call, it is a good idea to use a Script for the first while.

You may write it out exactly how you will say it, and how you will respond to predictable arguments. You may simply make notes of the key points or questions you want to be sure to touch on. Whatever you are comfortable with, do that. Many times the script will evolve as you use it. A script should always feel natural to you. Say it in your own way; your own words.

I have always found the easiest way to write a script is to imagine myself actually talking to someone. Pick someone specific to use in your mind as the person you are presenting the idea or conversation too. Speak to them in your mind. The script will flow naturally from this exercise.

After a short time, you will no longer need a script. You will be comfortable with your comments and responses and the conversation will happen automatically. However, use a script until you feel comfortable, or whenever you go back to do a project you've abandoned for a time.

CHAPTER 16

THE QUALIFYING QUESTION

Would you like this person to be your customer?

Is this person worth the time and effort you are going to invest to make them a customer? Find out how to design a qualifying question that will ensure everyone in your pipeline has the potential to be one of your best customers. Learn what questions you need to ask yourself that will enable you to know what qualifying question to ask. You are going to put a lot of effort into making this person your customer. Are they worth it?

Kick Start Checklist

- ✓ What is your qualifying question?
- ✓ Have you asked your qualifying question of everyone in your pipeline?
- ✓ Are they worth the effort you are going to put in to make them your customer?

CHAPTER 16

THE QUALIFYING QUESTION

In the last chapter, I referred to the "Qualifying Question" in our introductory script. I cannot emphasize enough the importance of qualifying the people who are going into your pipeline.

When you are relatively new in your business, you have more time for prospecting activities than you do in later years. In building my three clienteles, it was interesting to see how the use of my time shifted. In the early period, most of my contacts were first contacts. Then as my pipeline grew, more and more of my time was spent on follow-up calls and meetings. Then, of course, my clientele began to grow. After about 3 years, I was spending most of my time on managing my customer base and had to force myself to allocate time to prospecting activities.

When I am doing workshops for seasoned advisors and I ask them: "How many people do you have in your pipeline?" it is not unusual for them to tell me, "No one". This is amazing to me. What they are saying to me is that there is absolutely nobody that they would like to have as a new client. How can that possibly be?

If you are reading this book, you are doing so because you would like to find new customers just like your best ones. The busier and more successful you are, the less time you have available for prospecting activities. You must not waste valuable time working on an opportunity only to discover that either, you would not want this person as a customer, or that they could never be one.

"Think what one question you can ask that will qualify him or her to be one of your best customers."

This is where your qualifying question becomes so important. You must be able to capture, in one question, an answer that will tell you that this person has a need for you, and that you want him as a customer. Does a certain income qualify them? Net Worth? Type of asset base? Corporate structure? Family situation? Age? Make your question your advantage.

"The less time you have available for prospecting activities the more important it becomes to be sure you are qualifying the people you are spending your valuable time on."

Have you asked everyone in your pipeline your qualifying question? If not, make sure you do. There is a very good possibility that you will uncover some new opportunities.

"When did you last re-qualify everyone in your pipeline?"

Do not be afraid to re-qualify your pipeline regularly. You should be culling your pipeline regularly to ensure you are always spending your prospecting time on quality people, who have the potential to be your best customers. You should also be culling your customer base regularly, to free up time for prospecting activities, and improving your relationships with your best prospects and customers.

THE SUCCESS GRAPH

As you can see from the graph on the following page, the larger your customer base, the less time you have for prospecting activities.

"Your Time is Valuable!"

Make sure everyone in your pipeline is worth the time you are investing in them!

The Success Graph

Year 1   Year 2   Year 3   Year 4   Year 5

CHAPTER 17

THE RELATIONSHIP OF TRUST BEGINS

Do you promise not to sell them anything if they'll agree to meet you?

Find out how important it is to meet someone and how hard it can be to do so. Learn how the relationship does not start until you meet someone, and they willingly share the information you need to qualify them to be your customer. Discover the most powerful statement that exists to meet someone. Use this statement to meet people who have not been willing to meet you. There's an old saying "You can talk to someone on the phone for ten years and never get to know them, but you can meet them for ten minutes and feel like you've known them for ten years". Let me show you how to transform your relationships with strangers into a relationship of familiarity and trust.

Kick Start Checklist

✓ Have you promised everyone you would like to meet, that you will not try to sell them anything if they will meet with you?

CHAPTER 17

THE RELATIONSHIP OF TRUST BEGINS

A. TRYING TO MEET THE PERSON

The purpose of the First Contact is to qualify the person and capture them for your pipeline. Once the person is qualified, the only goal is to meet them.

"This is where the game begins!"

Many people will not want to meet you. They know! If they meet you, the relationship will change. You will become a person. You will no longer be just a voice on the telephone. For this to happen however:

"You must get the meeting!"

Many years ago, when I was building my first clientele, I volunteered on a community society in White Rock. In this group, there was a woman everyone said was very well to do.

Some time after my involvement with this group ended, I followed up and called Mrs. A. to introduce myself on a professional basis. She told me Mr. A. handled all the money. I called him and he was very nice yet firm. He had people helping him with his money. "Someone new would just create more paper," he said.

I asked, "Why don't we meet?"

He replied, "I don't want to. If I do, and I like you, we'll probably do business together. And I don't want that to happen."

Over a number of calls, I continued to press for a meeting. I said, "Come on. Meet me. I promise not to sell you anything. Just meet me. Let me be more than just a voice on the phone."

I used a line that I use over, and over again, with people whom I want to meet:

"I'm not trying to sell you anything. I would just like to meet you. There is an old saying that you can talk to someone on the phone for 10 years and not get to know them, but you can meet someone for 10 minutes and feel like you've know them for 10 years. I just want to meet you—I promise I won't try to sell you anything."

This went on for some time. Finally, he agreed to meet me. He ended up becoming one of my top 10 clients with over $3 million in holdings with me.

He knew that if he met me, our relationship would change. He was right! This is the secret to prospecting. Meeting people! This is the game! And make it that. A game. Believe it works, and try to have fun doing it.

B. "I PROMISE IF YOU'LL MEET ME I WON'T TRY TO SELL YOU ANYTHING"

It is very important to let people know that you are not trying to sell them something. Most people are very defensive about being sold something. They constantly have their guard up. Especially successful people, the kind you would like as customers. Everyone is trying to sell them something.

You must be different. You must show them you are not there to sell them anything. You must show them that you truly believe in, and want to build long-term relationships with them, and that you are not just trying to get the quick sale.

This can be especially difficult in the early years of building a customer base. You feel desperate sometimes. You really do need the sale. You want so much for them to do business with you.

As desperate as you may be, it is critical that you do not try to sell them anything before you meet them, or during your first meeting. If you do, you are violating the commitment you have made to them that unless you have a better understanding of their overall situation, you cannot honestly recommend anything.

Whatever service or product you offer, you cannot do the best possible job for your customers if you do not know enough about their situation to know what fits best for their unique situation.

People know this. If you offer them something too soon, they will see that you are just a "salesman" like so many others. When you specifically show disinterest in selling them something, it is very powerful. You are proving you are truly interested in them. Ready to accept it, if what you offer does not fit. Ready to be patient, if you discover that some day you might be able to be of service to them, but that time is not now.

Your only goal in meeting someone for the first time should be for each of you to discover whether, "somewhere down the road", you might be of service. Sometimes, "somewhere down the road" can be as early as the follow-up meeting, because there was a need for you and you connected right away during the meeting. Sometimes, it will be clear there is nothing that you will be able to do for the person in the near future.

Whatever the current need, at the end of this meeting, you will both have a clear understanding of if, or when, "somewhere down the road" you will be able to be of service.

I cannot emphasize enough that you really do not know someone until you meet him or her. The immediate "sales" opportunity is nowhere near as important as the building of your relationship with this person. You now have a clear understanding of who they are and when, if ever, they will have a need for you. They know who you are, and what you do. You have now become a person to them, and it is just a matter of time before an opportunity to make this person your customer comes about.

C. THE SECOND CALL

Your second call is to see if they received your introductory package, and if they will meet you. Many times, they will not remember you. Little do they know that your name, in time, will grow to be very familiar to them. All future calls have the same goal in mind–to meet them.

The conversation might go something like this:

*"Hi John! This is Doug Lachance of _____.
I spoke to you a couple weeks ago and promised to send you an introductory letter. Did you receive it?"*

If they did not, confirm their address and say you will send it again, and then diarize for 2 more weeks.

If they have received it, you try to get a meeting with them.

"Great! I was hoping we could meet each other. Is there a time next week which will work for you?"

If they answer yes, great! Away you go.

Once again, you do not have to make this follow-up yourself. Someone else on your team can do this for you, but the process is the same and must be done. Unfortunately, they will often not want to meet you. They know the relationship will change. They are busy, and they are happy. They are not interested in reviewing what they are doing with respect to your product or service, at this moment in time. They do not want to waste their time on a meeting which they can see no benefit in having. It will be one excuse after another.

You must be persistent without being annoying. You must be patient. The day will come when you will meet them. All you want, for now, is the invitation to get to know them better, and possibly, "somewhere down the road" you will be of service to them.

"The slow drip has begun!"

D. FOLLOW-UP CALLS

You will have to decide how frequently to call each individual prospect. Initially, it should be a very systematic process. It begins with the first call. As I previously mentioned, from that point on you must try to meet the person.

Many times on the second call, the person will not remember you. Other times, they remember you, but were not expecting you to call back, as they thought they successfully got rid of you on the previous call.

Sometimes the person will be happy and does not see the need to meet you. I like to respond with something like this:

> *"I know you're happy now, but situations change. You could become unhappy. Your advisor might leave the business or make a change. I just want to meet you so I will be more than a strange voice on the phone. Then, somewhere down the road, if your situation changes, you will know who I am. I promise if you meet me, I won't try to sell you anything."*

E. CALLING YOUR EXISTING PIPELINE

Have you met everyone in your existing pipeline? If not you should endeavor to do so. You need to "position" yourself with these people, even if they are happy at this time. Hopefully in this meeting you will get enough information to do a complete analysis. You can show them the wonderful job you could do for them, if they ever had a need for your product or service.

For anyone in your pipeline that you have met, but have not yet had an opportunity to show all you do, and the wonderful product or service that you have to offer, the following is a script I used to use. Try to adapt it to what you have to offer. Create one that will make someone want to tell you all about themselves.

> *"Hi John! This is Doug Lachance from _____."*

> *"John, I've been wondering - When was the last time you had a complete analysis of your situation done to be sure your retirement and estate planning are on track?"*

"We have some excellent tools at _____ to do a complimentary analysis for you. This includes an analysis of your risk profile, asset allocation as well as a retirement projection to see if your present savings and investment plans are on track to achieve your retirement goals. (If qualified you might also say: I can also analyze your tax situation and/or your estate requirements)"

"What I've found is that people really enjoy going through this exercise. It is a good feeling to know things are on track. If you do this exercise, I know you will find it extremely interesting. You'll confirm your present game plan is working or it'll provide you with a great roadmap for the future."

"The process involves a one hour information gathering meeting and about an hour and a half to review the results."

"Would you like me to do this for you?"

No matter the product, or service you have to offer, you want to position yourself with your prospect. The best way to do this is to offer something of value in the presentation of what you provide. What is the problem that you solve for your customers? Offering to review and /or analyze a prospect's circumstances will show them, and you, if they have a need for you, or when they might.

Once you analyze their situation, you will know when this need will arise. Is there a life event ahead that could change their present circumstance? You now have the information you need to position yourself perfectly for when 'Money goes in Motion'. Uncovering this future need, you can ask, "When _____ happens, may I be one of the people you give consideration to?" You will get a commitment for the future opportunity.

Another powerful result of an analysis and presentation is that you have presented your value proposition to them. You have shown them what you do, and they now know who you are. You are now competing with their present provider. You know their needs, and you can begin servicing them, even though they are not your customer yet! You will give them a sense of the service you would provide, if ever given the opportunity to do so.

Have you positioned yourself like this with everyone in your pipeline? If not, you should make every effort to do an analysis and presentation for each of them. You want to be a serious candidate for their business the next time 'Money goes in Motion'. You will not be, if they do not know who you are and what you do.

CHAPTER 18

ONGOING CONTACT

What are you prepared to do to help
your prospects get to know you better?

What strategies are you using to "slow drip" your pipeline? Do you send a newsletter regularly? When was the last time you sent an article of direct interest, with a personal note, to your best prospects? You must constantly be seeking ways that you can be building trust and familiarity with your prospects. Find out how to grow your relationships with a gentle and quality "slow drip". Learn how to help people get to know you better; to create a dynamic newsletter that captures your strengths and personality; the power of a personal touch in notes and correspondence; and how effectively to use the internet and email.

Kick Start Checklist

✓ Do you have a dynamic ongoing communications program?
✓ When was the last time you sent a hand written note to your best customers?
✓ What have you done lately to help your prospects get to know you better?

CHAPTER 18

ONGOING CONTACT

I believe that people grow to be familiar with you, from a distance, from the ongoing communications you are doing with them. E-mail and the Internet have created an incredible opportunity to slow drip. However, you must also try to personalize some of your contacts. You want these people to get to know you, and trust you.

I believe you must communicate with people in a quality, and direct way, at least 3 to 4 times a year. This can be a regular newsletter, a special mailing piece, or whatever. The most important thing is the quality of the ongoing contact. It is a bonus, when you are able to refer back to how often, and long, you have been in contact with someone.

One day, you will be able to say:

"... You know Bill, we have known each other for (1, 2, 3 etc.) years now. Don't you think it's time we met?"

Another important impact of the slow drip is to keep your name in front of the person. You want a familiarity to grow. You do not want to reintroduce yourself every year. The relationship will never grow if that is the case.

If you are using a wide variety of contact ideas and invitations, you may never know which one triggers the response you have been hoping for. Although many of your slow drip strategies will be information only, you should continually think of ideas that have the potential to trigger a connection. Knowing what that trigger is can be very important.

Perhaps it will be an invitation to a seminar they are interested in, or perhaps a tax idea. It might be something that gives you a reason to call them for further information. The very best opportunity to make a connection is an invitation to an event that will allow you to meet them in a non-threatening situation.

I believe it is important that you spend some money on your follow-up activities. You need what you are doing to stand out. You want the person to feel special, and that they are important and valuable enough to warrant your personal attention.

A good way to decide what to mail on a regular or special basis is to think about what you are trying to accomplish. Is it to announce a new product or service? Is it to simply make a quality contact and build the relationship? Is it to give them an insight into what makes you special? Think of something that will best catch their attention, and deliver your message.

However, if you are going to put the time and money into a communication project or strategy:

"Do it in a quality and professional way!"

What and how you send information to people will have on impact on what they think of you. Everything you do should be a stepping-stone on the path towards the opportunity for a full presentation of your product or service, and your value proposition.

The most important goal of a regular communication strategy should be for you, yourself, to capture the attention of someone on a regular basis. Their connection to you will grow, and along with it, a sense of familiarity and trust.

A. NEWSLETTERS

I really like a good newsletter. It provides a foundation of regular, consistent, personal contact. It forces you to have the discipline to coordinate a direct communication to your entire contact list on a predetermined basis.

Some people do monthly newsletters. I, personally, believe it's better to do a really great newsletter that is interesting and thought provoking less frequently, than to do one that is bland, repetitive and boring, more often.

Your newsletter is a great opportunity to let your pipeline get to know you. I always used lots of editorial comments and quotes as an insight into my personality and how I think.

I had always done a newsletter at least every 3 to 4 months, and I spent quite a bit of time on it. It was always professionally printed on quality paper (8 ½ x 11) and had 4 pages. To save costs I purchased the paper in bulk and left it with the printer. I had an artist design the letterhead and format, and it looked very elegant and professional. I believe its high quality, both visual and verbal, compelled people to stop a moment and read it. I always had many compliments on my newsletters and it was a great opportunity to ask if they know of someone who might enjoy receiving it.

My newsletter was constantly changing and evolving. I was always searching for freshness, and tried very hard to keep it from becoming boring. It was colorful and eye catching. I included quotes and short articles; editorial content and opinions written by me; and as well, added reprints of other interesting content.

I would keep a folder handy for newsletter items. Anytime I saw an article, quote, or anecdote that I liked, I would put it in the folder. When it came time to write my newsletter, I would go through the folder, and usually over half my newsletter was already done.

I have always believed that my newsletter gave my pipeline a feel for how I thought, and what was important to me. I like to think it made them think of me as informed, intelligent, and insightful, as well as being professional and competent. My newsletter was always a great way to contact everyone in my pipeline, every 3 to 4 months. It made a terrific contribution to the building of many long-term relationships.

B. PERSONAL LETTERS

I have always found that personalized letters are much more powerful then mass mailings. On occasion, I write a letter for distribution to my entire pipeline. I pick one person and write it specifically to him or her. What would I like to say to this person to help build this relationship? Or, perhaps, motivate them to want to meet with me? This would be the draft for the form letter for the whole pipeline. I always signed them, giving them a personal feeling.

Try to write at least one personal letter per year to your entire pipeline. More often if you can.

Handwritten notes, I believe, are the most powerful of all. For the person to know that you took the time to think specifically of them is a very powerful contact. Attaching an article of interest for them, exclusively, further enhances the impact of this personal touch. I am constantly trying to find out more about the people in my pipeline. What their interests are, and what is important to them. I am always on the lookout for some interesting or unique thing that will show I was thinking about them personally.

C. E-MAIL

E-mail has created a great opportunity to communicate cheaper and more efficiently. However, you have to be careful that you do not end up just being "spam". People could be deleting it without even looking at it or reacting negatively to it for any number of reasons.

There is nothing wrong with sending information to prospects this way; however, you should be careful what ideas you send to what people. In the investment business, sending information or an idea that is of no interest, or violates a person's investment objectives, could result in them writing you off in their minds.

Your e-mail strategy changes as your customer base grows. Once you have a large clientele, and are mostly managing them, you are primarily communicating ideas to people who want to receive them. E-mail is a great way to communicate with people who are looking forward to receiving information from you.

I believe that whatever e-mail activities you are doing, on a reasonable basis (at least two or three times per year) you should also be sending something by regular mail as this has a much more personal feel to it. This is where regular mail has an advantage. You can use strategies such as an eye-catching design that will make the person want to read your piece. Making it interesting, informative, and visually appealing can cause him or her to set it aside to read at their leisure and help them remember you in a positive way.

If I build another clientele, I will maximize my e-mail efficiency, but I will continue to use regular mail. At least every 3 months, I will personally prepare an eye catching, interesting, powerful newsletter that I will mail to everybody in my pipeline. By personalizing, putting in a visible effort and spending money from time to time, you consistently show people that they are valuable enough to you to be worth the costs..

"This is a great way for everyone to get to know you better and help your relationship grow."

CHAPTER 19

HOW TO GET THE MEETING

How do you meet someone who has no interest in meeting you?

Have you had difficultly in getting a meeting with your best prospects? Are they unreceptive because they are busy and hit on all the time? Learn how to break through. Wouldn't you love to sit down with people who have the potential to be your best customers, and get to know everything about them as they get to know you? Discover how to generate new business opportunities with the power of networking. Learn how to use it as an opportunity to meet your best prospects, and be introduced to new prospects.

Have you hosted a seminar recently? Seminars are a very effective way to meet prospects. Use the seminar worksheet to plan a seminar for your best customers, their friends, and others just like them. I will share with you the insights I have gained over the years, and help you choose a speaker that will make people want to come to your seminar.

Kick Start Checklist

✓ What activities are you doing to meet people?
✓ What networking activities are you part of?
✓ When will your next seminar be?
✓ Who will be your guest speaker?

CHAPTER 19

HOW TO GET
THE MEETING

A. NETWORKING

Networking is one of the most powerful customer building tools there is. It creates opportunities to make contact with people who are difficult to meet, and to meet others who you would like to have in your pipeline.

There are many ways to meet someone. Meeting one-on-one is ideal. Many times however, you will find it very difficult to meet a successful person. They are busy and hit on all the time. Often, they are happy with their present provider and do not presently have a need for you.

It is important to break through. To separate yourself from the many others, who constantly call to sell them something, you must meet the person. Their defenses will be up. They are used to blowing off people who are trying to hit on them. You must survive this initial, instinctive, and defensive reaction. Most importantly, you must make them willing to meet you, to see you as a person, and to start a relationship with you.

For a period of 3 - 5 years minimum, you should have at least 2 networking activities happening on an ongoing basis. These two can change or evolve, but you should always have at least the two happening.

There are a number of different types of networking activities.

1. SOCIAL NETWORKING—This automatic networking occurs when you are with friends and family. Personally, I try to avoid talking business on these occasions. If pressed, I will suggest we get

together another time to discuss it further. (Social networking does not count for your two networking groups.)

2. COMMUNITY ACTIVITIES (indirect–very powerful on a long-term basis)—Belonging to community organizations can be very satisfying as well as providing powerful long-term benefits. I have always tried to be active in the community. By being visible, in a non-business and contributing role, it gives people the opportunity to see you, and come to know you, for the person you are: your integrity, professionalism, and character. Over the years, the return for your efforts will come back to you in a powerful way, with the reputation you have earned for yourself.

It takes many years to build a reputation, and can be one of the most powerful influences on the new customer opportunities presented to you. It also can be very influential in people referring others to you. It has a very positive impact on the credibility, and the trust that will be in place in you during the analysis and presentation opportunities. A good reputation is easily the most powerful asset you can ever have. It is worth the effort it takes to build a great one!

I built my first clientele in Penticton, British Columbia. To the south of Penticton are two smaller communities, Oliver and Osoyoos. The trip from Penticton to Osoyoos takes about 45 minutes. It is a very pretty drive with many orchards, vineyards, and golf courses along the way.

I rented space in a small real estate office in Osoyoos, and made a commitment to visit every Thursday. I went out to the local golf men's night and attended community events from time to time, and the people became familiar with me. Three years later over 1/3 of my clients were either in or along the road to Osoyoos. I never tried to sell anything. Just attending these events, and having people get to know me personally, created the trust and familiarity. This is a great example of the long-term impact of community activities.

I believe it is extremely important to avoid using community activities in an aggressive business development manner. Your reasons for being there should be the cause represented, and you should direct all your energy to doing as good a job as you can. This will enable people to see you for the person you are.

I can remember times over the years where someone joined a group I was involved with, specifically to aggressively promote themselves or sell something. They were always gone quickly, and left a very unpleasant aftertaste in everyone's mouth. You would not want this to be you.

3. GROUP NETWORKING—A perfect opportunity to ask for a "get to know you" meeting—This is a networking activity where you have arranged, or are part of, a group that meets regularly to share common interests. The objective is to give value in a non-threatening, friendly environment. An example of this would be the "SUCCESS" group that I will discuss shortly.

You must use your imagination to create or join a network that potential customers would want to be part of. You must focus on their commonality. What would all or most of this group of people have in common?

If you are arranging it yourself, once you have the theme, you pick the date, choose the venue, prepare an agenda, and away you go. It is happening. Your first meeting is set. Now you start talking to people about it. If you have chosen the right idea, people will want to come.Putting on an event presents you in a very high profile manner. It gives you a great opportunity to meet people, some for the first time, in a pleasant and friendly setting, and it opens the door to "getting together for a coffee to get to know each other better" in a future call.

Again, the primary goal of all your activities should be to find and build long-term relationships. Over time, these long-term relationships will reward you with opportunities to provide advice and guidance to people you have come to know, and care about.

4. **MOTIVATED NETWORKING**—Helping each other get referrals.—A great and powerful networking activity is creating, or joining a group that is committed to providing each other with referrals. By finding the right individuals in each profession, you can create a very dynamic referral generating entity. Only those who give referrals are allowed to remain in the group. Everyone must be willing to give, to receive.

B. SEMINARS

Seminars are a wonderful way to meet new people, and to build trust and familiarity with existing people. Seminars can be big or small. Over the years, I have done hundreds of seminars. Some were small (10 to 20 people) on a specific topic; some were large (600 to 800 people) with a high profile speaker and the whole office involved. Seminars are a fantastic way to meet the friends and family of your existing customers. With the right theme, or guest speaker, a seminar can also act as a novel way to meet the prospects you have not yet met. Finally, if you have advertised your seminar, you will meet new people who have come because of your promotional efforts.

As I mentioned in an earlier chapter, taking 5 minutes and booking a room for 2 months down the road is a very positive way to get busy. Once you book the room however, you must do everything you can to make it a great event. Get good speakers. Send invitations. Follow up by phone. (Make a final reminder call to everyone) Get a good turn out. Then, you must make sure you put on a great event. Be there early. Make sure everything is set up and ready to go. Welcome people as they arrive. Have a door prize and critique sheets, so you can get everybody's name and contact info.

Alternatively, do a series of smaller seminars in your boardroom. Make them small, perhaps 10 to 15 people. Target your guest more specifically for a certain need or interest. You be the speaker. Show your knowledge and expertise. In addition to selectively inviting your best customers and their friends (and selectively, your prospects whom you know qualify to be there), you may advertise. Do a mail drop. Education can be a good magnet for potential new customers. People like to learn. Position yourself as their teacher and you will have moved them solidly along the relationship curve.

(A Seminar Planning Worksheet is on the following page.)

Doug E. Lachance

SEMINAR PLANNING WORKSHEET

1) **Who is your target group?**
   Identify the profile of the people you would like to have attend. (Retirees, business people, executives, professionals, etc)

2) **Choose your topic.**
   Think of one topic or more. A successful concept is to have more than one speaker. Perhaps have an expert on gardening (or other lifestyle topics) and an expert on a business topic (investing for income, tax strategies, RRSP's, etc).

3) **Book the Event.**
   Decide what kind of event you will have and book the room.
   What?—Breakfast; Lunch; Dinner; Coffee and Pastries.
   Where?—Restaurant; Hotel; Boardroom; School; Theatre.
   When?—Choose a date that will give you lots of time to be organized.
   Who?—Book your speakers.

4) **Promotion**
   Invitations; Phone calls; Direct Mail; Advertising; Press Release

5) **Follow up**
   Always confirm attendance a few days before

6) **Be Prepared!**
   Be sure everything you need will be there: Audio-visual equipment; adequate seating; refreshments; door prize(s)

7) **Handout Materials**
   Seminar Packages (marketing materials, speaker handouts); Agenda; Evaluation Questionnaires (It is important to capture the names of attendees. I would ask them to fill out a questionnaire and then, use those to draw the door prize.); Name Tags; Paper and Pencils; Business Cards

CHAPTER 20

SUCCESS IN STARTING A NETWORKING GROUP

"How would you like to belong to a club exclusively comprised of your best customers and their peers?"

"SUCCESS" was chosen as one of the "Great Ideas from Top Performers". Let me show you how reading a book, entitled "Selling to the Affluent" by Thomas J. Stanley, inspired me to create this networking group compromised exclusively of people who had the potential to be my best customers. Find out how to start your own networking group that will cater exclusively to your best customers and people just like them.

Kick Start Checklist

✓ Can you think of a networking group theme whose membership would consist exclusively of people just like your best customers?

CHAPTER 20

SUCCESS IN STARTING A NETWORKING GROUP

You must use your imagination to think of ways to break through. Following is a networking idea (SUCCESS) that I came up with, which enabled me to meet a number of people who had until then, not been willing to meet me.

Personally, I have found that in the investment business, a successful businessperson is the ideal customer. I once read that studies have shown the majority of millionaires are, or were, business people. Great customers can come to you from a myriad of other directions, but I have found the best prospecting focus to be successful business people for the following reasons:

1. Great Asset Bases - Buildings, Company, Financial Assets, etc.
2. Has an RRSP funded by maximum annual RRSP contributions (Many times a spousal RRSP as well).
3. Has a high income and cash flow.
4. Pays a lot of income taxes (and hates it!).
5. Is growth orientated.
6. Can evaluate risk.
7. Can understand a good idea.
8. Can make a decision.

In a great book I read called "Selling to the Affluent", by Thomas J. Stanley, he advised that successful people are constantly bombarded from all directions. One idea he suggested to overcome this obstacle, and meet these people, was to join the groups that are associated with successful business people. I considered the effort it would take to become part of so many organizations. The time and energy. What a daunting task!

Then I had an idea. Why not create a group. One whose membership would consist of exactly the kind of people I wanted as clients, with me organizing and coordinating the activities.

I thought up an acronym for "SUCCESS":

SHARING AND UNDERSTANDING THE COMMON CONCERNS OF ENTREPRENEURS AND SIGNIFICANT SHAREHOLDERS

I decided I would do early breakfast meetings, 7:00am. Early enough that attendees could be at work by 9:00am or shortly thereafter. For a guest speaker, I decided I would get one of their own—a successful businessperson whose success they might relate or aspire to. Some of my guest speakers included: Peter Thomas—Past Chairman of Century 21 (Peter has subsequently sold his interest). A number of my "SUCCESS" regulars told their stories. Most successful people love to share their success with their peers. They also enjoy visiting with people like themselves: common goals, similar problems, and interests. Try to think of other speakers whose expertise would be of interest to your best customers. Use your imagination. (I once had David Foot, Canada's leading demographer, as a guest speaker—before, by writing a number of popular books on demographics, he became quite well known.)

I remember the first SUCCESS meeting. Before the meal started, I went around the room and had everyone introduce him or herself. At the conclusion of the breakfast, I asked what they all thought. Would they like to do it again in the future? There were about 40 people and the reaction was very enthusiastic. One person though, stood up and commented:

"I really enjoyed myself. I think the meetings are a great idea. I have one question though—Doug. What are you doing here?"

The place broke up! "SUCCESS" turned out to be a great success. As I mentioned, many of the people who became part of "SUCCESS" eventually became my clients.

FINDING A WAY TO BREAK THROUGH

A real interesting thing happened when I was calling to invite people to the first "SUCCESS" meeting. The reaction to my call was entirely different. I was calling about something not related to my business. I was calling to talk to them about something of value to them. Rather than being defensive and aloof, people became noticeably warmer. I had successfully removed the barrier. They were not afraid that I was going to try to sell them something.

I think it is extremely important to think of ways to meet people in a non-threatening way. Hosting or being involved in a meeting, group, or a project is a great way to establish a personal relationship and begin a friendship.

"Use your imagination!"

Your biggest prospects are worth the extra effort to meet them. Creating a networking group to accomplish this will result in your meeting, and getting to know, some of your best prospects.

"Begin friendships with large prospects and one day they will become your best customers."

CHAPTER 21

HOW TO HANDLE THE MEETING

What would you like to know about this person?

A meeting is the beginning of a new relationship. Do you know what to do and how to handle the meeting when you finally get it? Let me show you how to prepare for the meeting. How to control the meeting and what questions to ask. Find out how to use a meeting to uncover new business opportunities. Discover how to position yourself by planting the seeds for a future opportunity, if one does not exist today.

Kick Start Checklist

✓ Have you created a checklist for your meetings to be sure you are always prepared?

✓ What is your list of important questions that need to be answered for you to know when 'Money will go in Motion'?

CHAPTER 21

HOW TO HANDLE
THE MEETING

A. ALWAYS HAVE AN APPOINTMENT

It is important to make an appointment for a meeting, and to confirm the meeting, before you show up. There is nothing more frustrating, discouraging, and time wasting, than going to a meeting and discovering that the person is not there or unavailable. Do not let this happen. Always confirm your appointment!

B. YOU ARE GOING TO BECOME A PERSON

Congratulations! You are about to become a person. The individual that you have been prospecting, for however long, is finally going to meet you. The most important thing that will happen today is that your relationship with this person will change significantly. More important than any product or service that you have to offer, will be the first impression this person has about who you are. He or she will look at how you present and conduct yourself, and these observations will have a lot to do with where this new relationship will go.

   The next time you speak to this person, you will notice a different tone in their voice, a familiarity that was not there before. The most important thing is that you have succeeded. You have accomplished the most important thing:

"You have met them!"

You now know who they are, what their situation is, and what their dreams and goals are.

"Moreover, they have met you!"

You are no longer a strange voice on the phone. You are now a person. The relationship has changed! Trust will now start to grow, and one day, when 'Money goes in Motion', you will get an opportunity to make them your customer.

As important as this event is from a relationship perspective, it is the amount and quality of information you come away with, from a business perspective that will have the largest impact on successfully converting this person into your customer.

C. INFORMATION IS THE GOAL

Your goal in every meeting should be to get as much information as you possibly can. Always remember:

"The more information you have,
the better your follow up and relationship building will be."

Sometimes, your first meeting will be one where you meet them, specifically, to find out more about them. Many times this is a 'feeling out' meeting. You have worked hard to meet this person and they have grudgingly set aside the time for this. Your persistence has paid off. The goal always should be to try to get enough information for an analysis and proposal, so that when you have an opportunity to do one, you will be well prepared.

The amount of information you get is a very good indication of where you are on the relationship curve. Sometimes, you will get all the information you need to do a complete proposal. Many times, all you end up with is a little more information to use as ammunition for your continued slow drip. Occasionally, the person will be cool and aloof. They do not intend to do business with you at this time, but they are willing to meet you, because they are curious.

D. IMPORTANCE OF INFORMATION

The more information that you have, the better the follow up, and slow drip you will be able to provide. As mentioned, your ideal situation will be to have obtained sufficient information to do a complete proposal.

If the meeting has occurred only because of your persistence, and you are aware that they do not wish to do anything at this point, accept it at that. The person has no desire or interest in putting the time and energy into a complete analysis. They have already told you that they are happy. They are not ready. Remember, most importantly:

"You Promised Not to Sell Them Anything!!"

You must make sure you honor this commitment. In fact, if during the meeting the person is pushing for recommendations, I will say:

"I promised that I would not sell you anything in this meeting. What I would like to do is take away with me the information I need about you. Then, I would like to think about what ideas would best fit you and come back with something that I think would perfectly suit you. Would that be okay?"

"If you're interested in me coming back to you with a good idea, would you like me to do a complete analysis of your situation?"

The more information you have the better your future slow drip will be. Perhaps interesting articles on an area of interest you have uncovered. Any financial information ideally positions you to come back at them, specifically targeting areas of interest or concern.

The better the information, the easier it is to show them your service and insight, and the better the slow drip!

E. BE PREPARED

There is an old cliché "You never get a second chance to make a first impression".

I believe this to be very true. The purpose of the first meeting is to turn the stranger on the phone into a real person. The first impression you give to this person will probably be the one he keeps for the duration of your relationship. Following are some Do's and Don'ts to help make that first impression a good one:

1. **Look Professional**

   Your clothes must be neat and tidy. Many years ago, a mentor once told me:

   "Always look at someone's shoes. You can always tell from their shoes how they are doing. If the shoes look worn and tired, they probably aren't doing that well."

   This has always stayed with me. I always own two pairs of dress shoes. One pair is my day-to-day pair. The other pair is brand new. Whenever I have an important meeting, or function, I wear my best shoes. When my day-to-day shoes get tired, I buy a new pair, my "old" new ones become my day-to-day ones, and my new ones become my special occasion shoes.

2. **Be Well Groomed**

   Your hair should be clean and tidy; your hands should be clean and your nails clipped; you should be sure you do not have body odor and that your breath is fresh.

3. **Be Prepared**

   Bring a notepad and pen. Be ready to ask if you can take notes if the conversation moves in a direction to support this request.

4. **Speak Slowly and Clearly**

   Relax. Make sure they can understand you. Do not use slang or jargon.

5. **Do Not Chew Gum**

   There is absolutely, nothing worse than this. (I cannot believe anybody who is reading this book would not know this, but "Hey! You never know!).

6. **Have a Firm Handshake**

   Make sure your handshake is not limp, nor so strong you hurt or intimidate. I believe a handshake offers great insight into a person's personality. Have a firm, confident, but sensitive grip.

7. Be Confident

Do not be cocky or arrogant. Do not come on too strong. Gently take the conversation in the direction you want it to go.

8. Be Warm but Not Overly Friendly

Let the other person lead the way. React to them. Be careful not to present a manner that they may not approve of.

9. Be Respectful

Show a respectful attitude, but not one of awe, or a feeling of being overwhelmed. This is most important. No matter how big the prospect is, you must make them feel they do not intimidate you. They should get the feeling you would be competent to handle their business.

10. Rise to Greet Them

If you are meeting someone at their location, most likely you will be escorted to them. When they are meeting you, be it at your place of business or somewhere else, always rise to greet them.

11. Be on time

Always leave yourself a buffer. Nothing is more disrespectful of a busy person's time, than being late.

F. THE BUSINESS LUNCH

Meeting someone over a meal or drinks is a wonderful way to connect with people. They are relaxed. If you are buying, it will make them feel special. (Interestingly enough, I find the prospect is often quite adamant about buying, or paying their share. Some people do not want to have any sense of any obligation to you. They still appreciate the gesture however.)

This may be a somewhat more relaxed atmosphere to meet in, but remember that it is still a meeting, and be careful. I am reminded of an article I read that talked about a survey of CEO's, and what they felt were the two biggest "no-no's" at a business meal were. They were:

1. **Being Rude to the Server.**
   This was #1. Never be rude to your server at a business meal. (Let us hope you are not rude at any time!)
2. **Being Late.**
   This was the other big no-no. Be on time. Leave early. Know where you are going to park, or leave enough time to do so. Being early enables you to choose the table, and be there to welcome them, and make them feel important when they arrive.

G. CONTROLLING THE MEETING

Your goal when you meet someone is to find out everything you can about them. The hardest and easiest thing to do is to get the person talking. The hardest because you must direct the conversation into areas of importance to you, or you will have wasted the opportunity. The easiest, because once you get people talking many times you cannot get them to stop. I have found that the best way to get someone talking is to get them talking about themselves. People love telling you about themselves, especially successful people! They enjoy talking about the journey to their success.

An easy way to start this conversation is to ask them questions about their career:

"How did you decide to do what you do?"

"Where did you go to school?"

"When did you get into this business (or career)?"

"How did you get from there to here?"

Ask them about their business. Successful people love sharing their success with others! Ask them about their lives. (For sample questions see the Information Form in Appendix 2—Forms). Using common sense and having a sincere interest in whatever the person's career path is all about, is a great way to get a conversation going. Be alert for opportunities to take the conversation in new directions.

Once you get the conversation going, you must gently try to steer it towards whatever area it is that you need to know about, to know if, and when, you might be able to be of service to them. Some people will tell you everything you want to know. Others will be more secretive. Get as much information as you can.

Once you begin talking about important things, ask if you may take some notes.

You should have three types of information gathering forms. The first should be blank paper. This is simply to jot down facts as they are mentioned. If the conversation warrants, you should also have a Customer Information form (see Appendix 2 - Forms) handy so you can get detailed information. The third type of form is the Analysis Worksheet, tailored for whatever analysis you need in your particular business. Personally, I would bring a zipped leather portfolio that holds an 8 ½ x 11 pad and compartments for business cards, forms, and questionnaires.

I always strive to get as much information as I can. If possible, I try to get enough information to do a complete analysis.

The ultimate goal is to get sufficient information, and a desire for a complete analysis. In the investment business, the absolutely best scenario is to walk out with your customer form entirely completed; all the answers to the questions to do a complete proposal; whatever statements or reports that is required to do an analysis and prepare a proposal for this individual.

The goal in this first meeting, regardless of the type of business you are in, is to get sufficient information, so you know whether your product or service is ideally suited to this person. Your best scenario is to walk away knowing you have exactly the right idea, or solution, for this person and sufficient information to open an account for them when they decide to become your customer. You will simply take this information away, and come back to them with the proposal that suits the needs they have outlined for you

Up to this ultimate information-gathering meeting, the goal is to get as much information as possible.

H. SOME OTHER IMPORTANT QUESTIONS

As we have discussed, the goal of a meeting is to get as much information as possible, and to position your self for the future. Much of this will be factual information: personal, historical, and financial. This is all great, but more importantly, you must find out who this person is. What are their hopes? Their dreams? Their fears? Their goals?

Once you get people talking, it is sometimes hard to direct the conversation into areas that are important for you without appearing rude. Having some soft questions ready to go at the slightest break (taking a breath—everybody has to breathe) can be a great way to steer the conversation in a new direction.

Some good questions to ask people to help steer the conversation in a new direction are:

- What drives you?
- Where would you like to be in 10 years?
- What are the most important things to you?
- What are your dreams?
- If you could have anything, what would it be?
- Do you worry about anything? If so, what worries you?
- What is your worst fear?
- What makes you the happiest?

- Tell me about your family. Are you married? Do you have any children?
- Where are they at in their lives?
- What would you like for them in life?
- What would you like your legacy to be?

Who this person is, who they really are as a human being, is the most information you can find out about anyone.

If you can find out what someone's values are, and what is most important to them, you will know how to position yourself to meet their needs.

I. PLANTING THE SEEDS

Although the primary objective is to get as much information as possible, it is critical that you plant the seeds for your future opportunity. If possible, you should try to get a commitment to do so.

You have promised you will not try to sell them anything. You must honor that commitment.

At the end of the information gathering process, it is time to elaborate on what you do. Earlier, during your initial introduction, you spoke briefly about yourself and your company. Now, it is time to talk about how you manage money (or whatever service it is that you provide) and to motivate the person to give you a presentation opportunity the next time they have 'Money in Motion'.

How the meeting has gone will determine how you expand on what you do.

As an Investment Advisor, I would end many meeting this way:

"Thanks John! I really appreciate your sharing this information with me. I'll keep it confidential, of course."

'One of the most important things for everyone to know is if their retirement goals are on track." (Insert your short value proposition statement)

"We have some excellent tools at _____ to do a complete analysis of your situation. I have found that people who

do this find it is a great way to see if everything's on track. They find it is a great exercise and an excellent roadmap for the future. Perhaps I could do this for you at some time in the future?"

Sometimes they say yes. If they do, ask them when would be convenient to get the information you need to do it for them. Sometimes they will want to give you the information right away. You should make sure you always have your questionnaires or information gathering forms available. Other times, they are receptive but do not want to waste their time right now because they do not foresee 'Money in Motion' for some time.

J. GET A COMMITMENT

"Always Try to Get a Commitment for the Future!"

To get a commitment from them, try something like this at the end of your visit:

"Great. Thanks again John. Let's stay in touch. I will call you now and then and send you things from time to time. Should there be a time in the future when you have a need for what I do would you give me an opportunity to show you what I could do for you?"

I have always found that whenever you defer the decision to the future, people will usually agree with you. In doing so, they are giving you permission to stay in touch in case such a situation occurs.

You have now positioned yourself as a professional ready to show them what you can do should the need arise.

You Must be Patient!

It is just a matter of time before you will get the opportunity. Sometimes it happens right away. Other times it takes a little while for them to become dissatisfied with how their current provided is servicing them. Perhaps, a major event needs to occur in their lives in order for them to consider your product or service.

Eventually though your time will come. You will get an opportunity to present your value proposition and land a new customer.

CHAPTER 22

THE SECRET TO LANDING NEW CUSTOMERS

Are you ready to seize the moment?

Have you noticed that you usually only get one chance to land a customer? Something that separates top producers from everyone else, is knowing how to land a customer when given the opportunity. When the time comes that your prospect has 'Money in Motion', you must not blow the opportunity—you must seize the moment. There are four critical moments on the way to landing new customers—let me show you a process that will result in your landing your customers almost every time you are given the opportunity to do so.

Kick Start Checklist

✓ What are the four critical moments that will land the customer every time?

✓ Are you ready to seize the moment?

CHAPTER 22

THE SECRET TO LANDING NEW CUSTOMERS

A. THE FOUR CRITICAL MOMENTS

I believe there are four distinct moments that occur as someone moves along the relationship curve on the way to becoming your customer. They are:

1. Becoming the Face Behind the Voice
2. Getting to Know Each Other
3. Detailed Information Gathering
4. The Presentation and Proposal

Many times these four distinctive moments happen in separate meetings. Sometimes however, accomplishing the goals and objectives of more than one will happen in a single meeting. That is great, and it is certainly something to strive for. Regardless of how many times you must contact or meet your prospect, you want to make each of these four moments happen with them. Once you have:

"They will become your customer!"

So that you will clearly understand what these four critical moments are, and how to manage them, following is a description of each. Remember, these critical moments do not need to happen in separate meetings.

1. Becoming the Face Behind the Voice

FIRST MEETING: BECOME A FACE BEHIND THE VOICE

Process	Activities
Find a way to meet the people in your pipeline • Phone Calls • Letters • Networking • Seminars • Community Service • Fund Raisers	• Confident friendly smile • Firm handshake • Warm Greeting • Acknowledge how long you've been calling them • Tell them how pleased you are to finally meet them
Goals	**Action**
• Meet someone for the first time • Become a person to each other	• Ask them if you can get together sometime so you can get to know each other better

---

Once you have qualified and captured someone in your pipeline you will begin calling them and trying to move the relationship forward. Over time, a familiarity will grow with this name. Call by call, you will learn a little bit more about this person.

The first critical moment is the first time you meet each other face to face. At this moment, you become the face behind the voice on the phone. You become a person to each other.

At some point, you will meet them for the first time. This can be by accident, or it can happen because of a planned activity such as a networking event or seminar. However, it happens, at that moment **you will instantly recognize each other's name.** It is also at this moment, that you will become a 'person' to one another. Up until now, you have only been a voice on the phone to each other. You have imagined what each other looked like. Now you know. From now on, every time you speak to this person on the phone, they are going to *know* who you are. They may not know a lot about you yet, but you have become a person to them.

Once again, although you may not have an opportunity to gather information of any kind, you have accomplished the most important objective of all:

"You have met them!"

This is also an excellent opportunity to try to arrange the second critical moment. The second type of meeting is prearranged. This is the "Getting to know you meeting".

"You know _____, I've been calling you for _____ now. It is great to finally meet you. What would you think about getting together for a coffee or something some time so we can get to know each other a little better?"

"Rarely will someone ever refuse a request made face-to-face."

Now it is up to you to follow up. Call the next day. Make the appointment. Coffee, lunch, whatever is appropriate for this individual.

2. Getting To Know Each Other

SECOND MEETING: GETTING TO KNOW EACH OTHER

Process

- Make an appointment for the meeting
- Confirm the meeting
- Meet with the prospect
- Gather information
- Planting the seeds
- Follow up note

Goals

- Re-qualify the prospect
- Position yourself
- Get a commitment

Activities

Ask your prospect questions about:

- Family / Health
- Hobbies / Activities
- Career / Work
- Finance / Money
- Hopes / Fears
- Goals / Dreams

Action

Is there a fit with you?

- Are they ready to meet again (third meeting)?
- Would they like to do the third meeting now?
- Ongoing dripping until they are ready to move to the third meeting.
- When should you follow up? (Diary note)
- Thank you note. (Great to meet you!)

The second meeting: **"Getting to know each other"**, has usually been prearranged. Both of you has an objective: to get to know each other better.

This second meeting is more important than the first. In the first, you will become the face behind the voice, but in the second, you will truly become a person to each other.

It is in this meeting that they will tell you something about themselves; who they are and what is important to them. You will also get a sense of when, if ever, you might be able to be of some service to them. You will have an opportunity to present yourself as a professional at whatever you do.

"You have become a professional!"

They may not be ready to share all the details of their situation with you, and are meeting you with the intention of just 'get to know each other better'. They may not tell you much about themselves. Even so, this meeting is very valuable, as you will have a better understanding of who they really are. You may decide, regardless of their potential size, that you would never want them as a customer.

Most of the time, what will happen is that you will leave the meeting with a very good understanding of where you are at with them on the relationship curve, and can follow up accordingly. In this meeting, how much information you obtain will determine how you slow drip them, and how you will position yourself with them.

Sometimes, the first and second meetings happen concurrently. This happens anytime you are meeting someone for the first time, and at the same time, you have the opportunity to talk one on one. In such a case, each of you has the opportunity to get a sense of whether "somewhere down the road" you might be able to be of service to them.

"Get to know them!"

This is your chance to familiarize yourself with the person's situation, desires, and needs. At the same time, they will become familiar with you, your personality, qualifications, background, and services. This is also the time, when you will "plant the seeds" and position yourself with them for when 'Money goes in Motion'.

3. Detailed Information Gathering

THIRD MEETING: DETAILED INFORMATION GATHERING	
Process	**Activities**
• Make an appointment for the meeting • Confirm the meeting • Meet with the prospect • Obtain information	• Obtain whatever detailed information you need to analyze the person's situation to know what products and services that you offer would be best for them. • Complete all questionnaires for analysis
Goals	**Action**
• Provide an overview of your Review/Analysis and Proposal Process • Gather information required for Review/Analysis and Proposal	• Make an appointment to do the presentation of your Review/Analysis, Value Proposition, and Proposal

The third critical moment is the "**Detailed Information Gathering Meeting**". In this meeting, the person is motivated and interested in your opinions and advice regarding their situation. They realize that for you to analyze their situation, and come back to them with results and a proposal, they will need to share with you all of their relevant information. They are giving you an opportunity to show your value proposition and, if they like what they see, they are ready to do business with you because *'Money is about to go in Motion'*.

Once again, the second and third moments can occur in the same meeting. This meeting could be more than just getting to know you. This would happen if, when the person agreed to the appointment, he or she were prepared to give you the information. It is possible for the first, second and third moments happen at the same time. You might be meeting them for the first time, getting to know them better as a person, and getting all the information you need to do an analysis and presentation. An example of this would be if the person were referred to you, and coming to see you, specifically to see what you might do for them.

4. Presentation and Proposal

FOURTH MEETING: THE PRESENTATION AND PROPOSAL

Process	**Activities**
• Make an appointment	Present your Value Proposition
• Confirm the appointment	1. The Introduction
• Do whatever work needs to be done to prepare your presentation	2. The Analysis
	3. The Recommendations
• Meet with the prospect	4. Follow up
• Follow up	

Goals	**Action**
This is the meeting where you will show the prospective customer:	• Are they ready to move forward with you?
	If Yes:
• Your Value Proposition	• Begin the process of making them your customer
• How you are the best person with the best solution to their need	If No:
	• When would they like you to follow up?

The fourth meeting is your **Presentation and Proposal Meeting.** In many situations, it has taken a long time, sometimes many years, to position your self for this opportunity. When it finally comes, you must be ready to land the customer. You do not usually get a second chance. The secret to landing big customers is to have a value proposition, proposal template, and dynamic presentation that will land the customer, when given the opportunity to do this exercise for them.

The person may want to become your customer during the third meeting. They have told you everything about themselves, and they have decided they want to be your customer. How you move forward will depend on your product or service. In the investment business, I have always believed you cannot make an appropriate recommendation until you have analyzed the person's situation. If they wanted to become my client before this, I would open the account, and get the wheels in motion but then make another appointment to specifically share my recommendations with them. I wanted them to see I had put a lot of effort and thought into what I was recommending as the best solution for them.

B. SEIZING THE MOMENT

In the Investment business, you usually only get one chance to land a new client. When you finally get the opportunity, you must bring them home.

"Will you get a second chance if you blow it the first time?"

For someone to give you an opportunity to be one of the people to review their situation and do a presentation, there are three primary factors.

The first is trust. Over time, they have come to trust and believe in your integrity and ability through phone calls, meetings, and mailings. Alternatively, the trust could be there from another source; a referral from their family, friends or business associates. However it has been gained, trust is the most important part of the process.

The second is their desire to see how you would meet their need, if given the opportunity to do so. For some time, you have been talking to them about the possibility of you being of service to them at some time in the future. They are curious about what you have to offer.

The third, of course, is that they have a need for your services for some reason (which will emerge in the information-gathering component). Many times, 'Money is going in Motion' and it is forcing them to think about their financial situation.

"Are they ready to move forward?"

C. YOU ONLY GET ONE CHANCE

Earlier, I said that I believe that you only got one chance to make a first impression. I believe the same is true with the 'Presentation'. You usually only get one chance. The way in which your proposal is conducted and presented is easily as important as the proposal itself. You want to have effectively landed the customer and know that one day their business will be yours to manage.

This does not mean that they will give you the business right away. There are many reasons why it takes time for customers to transfer their business to someone new. This is a big decision for them. Provided you have done a good job in your presentation, there is a good possibility that some day, even if it is not today, their business will be yours.

If you blow this opportunity many times you will not get a second chance. All the work you have done to date, leading up to this moment, will be lost. It happens.

I remember once getting a referral from an accountant. We had talked about this referral for years. Finally, I was given the opportunity— a $2 million dollar referral. During the first meeting everything seemed to be great, in fact in hindsight, it was too good. It went so well that I got sloppy. Overly friendly, and overly confident. We talked about our backgrounds and got to know each other. I explained our investment process and talked about doing an analysis of his situation.

Instead of portraying the aloof professional, I was buddy-buddy. He responded great, or so it seemed. Something went wrong. I do not know exactly what it was, but for whatever reason, he never followed through with the exercise. I had taken him for granted and I never got a second chance.

There are many ways to ruin your opportunity.

I remember prospecting someone who said to me:

"I like your company. One of the Advisors from your office did a proposal for me once".
"Really? What happened? Why didn't you come over?" I asked.
"Well, I really liked the proposal, but it came in the mail and he never followed up".
I said, "You're Kidding!"
"Nope" he replied.
"I asked, "Was this the same amount as we are talking about now (over $1 million)?"
"Yes" he answered.
"Wow! I guess they kind of dropped the ball."
His response was "I suppose.".

Isn't that unbelievable! To do a proposal for a $1 million dollar plus account, mail it, have the person like it, and then not follow up!

WOW!!

When you finally get your big chance, the way your proposal is conducted, presented and followed up on is just as important as the proposal itself. You don't want to blow the opportunity you've worked so long and hard to get!

D. THE PRESENTATION

Just going through the exercise of doing the proposal and presentation, positions you wonderfully with the prospective customer. During your presentation, they see you at your best: smart, knowledgeable, professional. You are superbly positioned as an expert, and a teacher, as you move them through the presentation process.

Once you have done a presentation for someone, your relationship will never be the same again. It is at this time that the person has finally seen what it is exactly it is that you do. Up until this moment, they have had their own ideas about you. Their ideas, good or bad, may have been influenced or prejudiced by previous experiences in your industry. Now they know exactly what you do, how you do it and what you may do for them.

"Seize the moment!"

Your presentation must give them the confidence that you are the best person, with the best firm, and that you have the best plan and tools available to provide them with the product or service they require.

They must be confident that you can provide and monitor the results they want, and need, to provide them with the long-term security and peace of mind they are looking for.

CHAPTER 23

THE VALUE PROPOSITION

What is it that makes you special?

Do you know how to articulate your value proposition?

To create a presentation template that will land the customer every time, you must have a value proposition that captures who you are, what you do, and why this person should do business with you.

Do you know what it is that makes you special? If you do not know, or cannot express it, how are you going to communicate it to someone who wants to do business with you?

Let me show you how to identify your value proposition and articulate it so you may capture it in your presentation template.

Kick Start Checklist

✓ Have you completed the Value Proposition worksheet in Appendix 2?
✓ Can you articulate what it is that makes you special?

CHAPTER 23

THE VALUE PROPOSITION

You will start to build your presentation template by deciding what tools and products will be part of the exercise, and what word template you will use as the foundation, but driving the whole process must be a value proposition. The best way to describe this is to share with you what my value proposition was.

My Value Proposition was to:

- Firstly, show the people that I truly cared about them.
- Secondly, have them trust that I would always honor the investment objectives that were established, by and for them.
- Finally, fill them with the confidence, that I had the right tools, products, and strategy to execute the plan for them.

Another part of my Value Proposition was to show people that investing, from their perspective, could be simple. I would help them understand the most important things: the rate of the return, their risk tolerance, and the asset allocation strategy that best suited their situation and personality. I would then show them how I was the one who could best 'quarterback' the process, and help them to achieve their dreams and goals. I promised them that although some of the investment terms and concepts we would talk about may be hard to understand, I would always ensure that they understood, in simple terms, how every investment worked, how it fit for them, and why.

A powerful component of my value proposition was to show the client an outcome that would perfectly match their needs, and objectives, from both a portfolio design perspective, and a management style perspective.

A unique part of my value proposition was that my clients always understood, in simple terms, what strategy and investment types we were using, and why they are the best fit for them. I would show them not only what the best investments for them were, but more importantly, I would outline a method of managing their money. I would show them how it was unique because I was the integral ingredient in making it happen for them.

I added value by making it simple for my clients. I helped them understand, in as simple a way as necessary, within their personal capabilities. They always understood their risk profile, what ranges of returns were available within their profile, and in simple terms how these asset classes and investments worked. The client always determined, to some extent, the depth to which I would go. Some people want to know how they are being taken care of, but most people just want to know that they are being well taken care of. I try to make a point of never talking over a client's head—if you do so, they get confused and frightened.

You need to find what it is about you that adds special value. What makes you unique? Of course, you need to include your experience and qualifications, testimonials and other important information about your company and service, but most of all, you must find something that makes you, of all the people who do what you do, the best person for them to work with. Is it your work ethic? Your commitment to service? How you do what you do?

"How do you add value?"

This is applicable to whatever product or service you have to offer. Not only should your product or service be something this person needs, and wants, you should be an integral part of the decision. A confidence and trust that you won't sell them something that is expensive, or unnecessary, but instead have their best interests at heart. Knowing that your character, expertise, and integrity are exactly what will ensure that they get exactly what they need, at the right price.

You need to find your own personal value proposition. What makes you special? Why should people want to work with you? The template that you build will reveal your value proposition to potential customers.

What is it about your product, or service that will improve or enhance this person's life? What is it about your company that makes it different from the competition? What is it about you that makes you the ideal candidate to be this person's provider?

Do you know:

"What is it that makes you special?"

Once you have determined all the things that make you special, you must now incorporate all of the answers into your presentation template. The goal of your presentation is to have it showcase your value proposition. The presentation should naturally flow into a proposal of how your services will ideally meet their needs, and the objectives, that you have discovered in the information gathering process.

It must also capture what makes you special: why you, of all the people available, are exactly the right person with exactly the right strategy and products to perfectly meet this persons stated needs, goals, objectives, and personality.

Finally it will answer the most important question of all:

"Why should this person want to do business with you?"

(The questionnaire in Appendix 2—Forms, will help you answer this question. Some of the answers to these questions are factual in nature: "Our product or service is the best because...". Some of the most important answers, however, are much more subjective: They are about you, who you are, and how and why you do what you do.)

CHAPTER 24

THE PRESENTATION

*Have you got a presentation
that will land the customer every time?*

Your presentation template is simply, the most important factor in your success. Most of the time, you only get one chance to land the customer. How can you be sure, when the opportunity comes, you have a powerful and dynamic template that lands them every time?

Let me show you the four basic components of a dynamic presentation:

1. Overview: What and how you do what you do.
2. The Analysis: A complete review of the person's situation.
3. The Recommendation: Why you and your value proposition are the perfect solution for this person.
4. Follow Up: How should you end your presentation?

Kick Start Checklist

✓ Have you built a presentation template that captures everything about you, your company, your product or service, and your value proposition?

✓ Have you practiced your presentation to be sure that it is dynamic, comprehensive, professional, and yet easy to understand?

✓ Do you plan to use the "Two Meeting Process" to deliver a powerful presentation?

CHAPTER 24

THE PRESENTATION

A. THE KEY TO YOUR SUCCESS

Your 'Landing the Customer' presentation template is, perhaps, the most important of all your business activities. It has to be good enough that when given the opportunity to do so, you land the customer. You do not want to spend years building a pipeline, and then not be able to land customers when the opportunities come. If your proposal template is sensational, and they trust you, and have confidence in your ability to quarterback the process, you will usually land them.

When they are ready to take the time, most people enjoy finding out how you might be able to help them. The exercise provides them with the affirmation and comfort of a job well done, or it provides them with a solution to a perceived problem.

There have been many instances where I have found large investors who have never had an analysis done, or have not had one done for a long time. Many times, advisors become lazy with clients they have had for a long while. They become complacent. They are no longer doing the things that enabled them to land the client in the first place.

This is human nature. Whatever business you are in, you can be sure that some of your competitors' customers (and maybe some of your own?) are not receiving the service that they once did. Almost all of us get complacent to some degree as we become successful.

Are your competitors doing as good a job as they should? Your presentation, whether competing against an existing provider or one of a number being considered, must highlight you in such a way that you stand out from amongst the others. At the end of your presentation, you want it to be extremely clear that you are the perfect person to provide what is needed for this person's situation.

B. THE TWO-MEETING PROPOSAL PROCESS

I believe that regardless of your product or service, you should try whenever possible to have two meetings to present your value proposition.

The first meeting is to learn everything about the person that is relative to what you have to offer. You need to take this information away, so you can use it to prepare your proposal. Making a presentation, and not being aware of all the factors that could have an impact on your recommendations, could make you look foolish and unprofessional if uncovered during the presentation itself. Most likely, you will not get the business, and probably, you will not get a second chance either.

"Be sure you have all the information you need to make the right recommendations the first time!"

Next, you need to take the information and input it into your template. The result will be a beautiful, professional, bound proposal with support information, analysis, recommendations, and value proposition.

There is a great effort in building a great presentation template. Once completed however, most of the work is done forever. Afterwards, it usually only takes 15 or 20 minutes to input the new customer information, and Voila, it looks like you put many hours into the proposal.

To have a dynamic and powerful presentation:

"You must have a dynamic template!"

One major reason you want to have a second meeting it that you want the person to be fresh and alert for your presentation. The information gathering process can be long, and is quite tedious. You do not want them to be tired during your presentation.

"Get them excited about the work you are going to do for them!"

They will look forward to the presentation meeting and will be waiting to see what it is that you can do for them.

C. THE PRESENTATION

This is the big one! This is your opportunity to show the person why they should become your customer. You should design your presentation so it moves along quickly and smoothly, and does not go on for too long. If your presentation lasts too long, your prospective customers' eyes will glaze over and you will lose them.

I cannot emphasize enough how important it is:

"When given the opportunity, your presentation must be good enough to land the customer!"

I believe there are four basic steps in building a proposal template:

1. The Introduction

The introduction is your opportunity to lay a foundation for the recommendations that follow. You should discuss 'the big picture' and how your product or service fits within it. You should use whatever information or articles you have that support your overview, and verbalize your understanding of their situation and what needs to be done. Additionally, you should review your customer's needs, and undertake to provide any further information, and materials, that supports how your product or service will exactly meet those needs. You should use whatever information or articles that support your overview and verbalize your understanding of their situation and what needs to be solved.

It is always a good idea to help the person relax. One way to do this is to use humor here and there. I am reminded of a cute story I like to use at seminars, as well as at presentations, when discussing the importance of asset allocation and risk tolerance. It goes like this:

I had a client come in to see me one day. He was quite old. I was explaining the history of the markets, the importance of asset allocation and so forth when he said to me:

"I want 100% growth."

"100% growth!" I said. "Are you sure?"

"You bet!" he replied. "That's where the best returns are."

"What about risk? Volatility? Aren't you concerned about the value of your portfolio going up and down dramatically?" I asked him.

"What do you mean?" he replied.

"Let me give you an example." I said. "How would you feel if your portfolio dropped 25% in one week, like what happened in the crash of '87?"

"I'd sleep like a baby." he replied.

"Like a baby?" I said in astonishment.

"You bet!" he said. "I'd wake up screaming 3 or 4 times every night!"

I've always liked that story. Laughter is a great way to help people relax, and in my case, in the investment industry, it really reinforced the importance of asset allocation and understanding risk tolerance. Whatever your business, try to think of a story that will help them to relax.

2. The Analysis

What tools do you have available that can identify a need, and lead to a solution, to follow in your recommendation? In my business, I would perform an asset allocation analysis and explain how where the assets are allocated accounts for over 90% of a portfolio's performance. As well, I would perform a retirement projection to see if their investments would meet their future needs and dreams.

Are you using all the tools available to you? It amazes me, when I do workshops, to discover that many people are not using the tools available to them. Find out what tools you have available. Take the time to become familiar with them, and see how you can use them to create an analysis that you can include in your proposal template.

Perhaps you do not use analysis tools in your business. Real Estate and Auto Agents would be an example of industries where tools are not necessarily part of the analysis. Instead, your analysis might consist of a list of their needs and wants relative to the amount of money they have available.

*"The more comprehensive your analysis is,
the more powerful your recommendation will be."*

3. The Recommendation

Now is the time to provide a solution to your prospective customer's need. You have laid a foundation in your Introduction; you have supported the recommendations to follow in your Analysis; and now it is time to showcase the solution and your products and services that are part of that solution.

To do this you must:

a) Describe the products and services you offer, making sure to support them by reviewing the key ingredients of your Introduction and Analysis.

b) Share with them the strengths of your company; why you work for them and why they are the best company to provide the desired solution. Show them the additional services that are available to them as a customer.

c) Highlight your Value Proposition. How you do what you do? What will you do for them? Why are you the best person to work with them? What are the commitments you will make to this person? Who is your team? What is your background? What is your philosophy? What is it that makes you special?

d) Discuss the cost of doing business with you. Don't be afraid to talk about the costs associated in working with you. Don't brush them aside. If you have value to offer, be proud of the costs of working with you. Are you worth it? I always felt I was worth it, and was very upfront about what it would cost to work with me.

e) Provide them with testimonials from happy customers. This is absolutely the most powerful component of any proposal. Which current customers would be happy to give you a reference? Find them and ask if they will provide a written testimonial, or be available to speak to a prospective customer.

4. Follow Up

Prospective clients may be somewhat overwhelmed by the comprehensive review and proposal process. For that reason, I try to keep my presentation to a reasonable length of time. It always amazes me how quickly it goes by.

After I have finished my presentation, and answered any questions that may arise, I back off. I have covered a lot of ground, and the person needs to go away and digest all the information they have been given. I would explain this to them, and ask them: "When would you feel comfortable with me following up with you?"

This will tell you where you are with them. Sometimes, they will want to complete any necessary paperwork and get the process going right away. Other times, they will make an appointment to do so later. Perhaps they will advise you when their 'Money in Motion' event will be occurring, so you may be of service to them at that time.

However, there will be times when, no matter how well you have done your presentation, they are just not ready to make a change yet. This has never bothered me. I understand that most people do not like change, and I do not push. I know that my presentation will make them want to become my client; it is only a matter of time.

A decision on "When may I follow up?" is how I always finish this meeting. I let them pick the appropriate time, and then I make sure to follow up then. If they are not ready to do anything, I ask "Why". Don't be afraid to ask this. The work you have done for them so far, has earned you the right to ask this. Say something like, "Do you mind if I ask why you don't want to move forward?"

Whatever the reason, do not be discouraged. If the person trusts you, if what you have to offer is truly of value to them and you have presented it in a dynamic, powerful manner…

"One day they will become your customer!"

CHAPTER 25

A SPECIAL WORD: MOMENTUM

"Success is 10% inspiration and 90% perspiration."
- Thomas Edison

Whether you are new to your business, or a seasoned producer, you need to attract new customers if you want your business to grow.

Let me show you how to find the time to channel some new energy into a new direction. Right away, you will begin to see improved results. Within a short time, you will create a momentum that will translate into an ongoing stream of new customers, and rising income or revenues. Once in place, momentum is a powerful thing.

Kick Start Checklist

✓   How much momentum do you have?

CHAPTER 25

A SPECIAL WORD: MOMENTUM

A. FOR NEWCOMERS

If you are brand new to your business, I know how overwhelmed you are feeling. The first couple of years will be a grind, but also, a blur. For the first while, you will be stumbling around without the experience, and the confidence, that only comes with time.

You will make a lot of mistakes. You will blow opportunities that are presented to you. You will be discouraged; frustrated; tired. Many of you will give up. For those that do not, the survivors, believe in your pipeline. Visualize it.

"Day by Day, Week by Week, Month by Month, Year by Year Contact by Contact... Your pipeline will grow!"

And one day, you find you are busy managing a customer base of people who were, at some time, captured into your pipeline, and eventually, became your customer. Your pipeline will continue to grow, and will provide you with a steady stream of presentation opportunities. Referrals will create an energy all of their own, and you will be continually adding new customers.

The good news is:
"It's just a lot of hard work."

The bad news is:
"It's just a lot of hard work."

B. FOR MATURE BUSINESSES

If you are a mature business, you are probably very busy managing your existing customer base. If you are reading this book, it is because you want to add some new customers. To channel some energy in a new direction you must allocate the time to do so. More importantly, you must honor this commitment.

Make the time! Make it happen!

How much of your time are you prepared to devote to this? 10%? 20%? 30%? You must translate this into real time. Do you normally work 40 hours per week? Are you going to donate 20% of your time to new business development activities? Ok. That is 8 hours per week. Book it into your schedule. Use the time to create your introductory letter and presentation template. (Do you already have one? Set aside time to review it. Is it as good as it should be?)

Allocate time for new business development activities: mailings, seminars, networking activities, a newsletter, and telephone calls. Set aside the time to make calls and meet the people who are in your pipeline. Use call sheets to keep track of your efforts. Force yourself to use the time and make the calls, or hire someone to do this for you.

To build your customer base, you must do two simple things:

1. Set aside time for activities that will build a pipeline of people, just like your best customers.
2. Follow the process, and methods, described in this book to use effectively the time allocated for new activities.

C. THE BIG PICTURE

"People become what they expect themselves to become".
— *Mahatma Gandhi*

I have always been able to visualize; where I wanted to go, and what I wanted to do next. This ability has allowed me to successfully build 3 separate clientele's. It is my hope that in these few pages, I have inspired you to create your own vision, and given you the tools to make to happen.

One of the most important ingredients to create success is energy. You must create your own positive energy and channel it in various directions. If you focus your energy on a project, and do it well, you will succeed.

At the beginning of any new project, the energy is almost all outgoing. You may be working long hours, and not see any immediate results, but you must carry on. What you can see is the number of good prospects in your pipeline growing, and you relationships with these people improving.

With time, the energy you have spent will come back to you. You will be busy. Not because you are making yourself busy, but because, other people are making you busy. People are returning your calls. People are calling you, instead of you always calling them. You will be busy managing your business, and more new business will coming at you.

With each clientele I built, the first few years were grind, grind, and grind - all outgoing energy. Then it would begin to shift direction. The momentum would continue to build, and a point would come, where I simply had to show up, and be busy, to be making a lot of money.

It is an incredible feeling when this transition occurs in your business. The concepts discussed in this book are the ones I would implement, if I decided to build a fourth clientele. Even if I do not, I have found that applying these same principles to other projects yields similar results.

If you are ready to believe, and if you are prepared to work harder then you've ever worked before, I know that the fundamental principles and process discussed in this book will not let you down.

"Your teacher can open the door, but you must enter by yourself."
— *Chinese Proverb*

APPENDIX 1

KICK START CHECKLIST

KICK START CHECKLIST

Chapter 1
✓ What are the 'Money in Motion' events unique to your business?

✓ How are you going to position yourself for when 'Money goes in Motion'?

Chapter 2
✓ Why do you choose a product or service?

✓ What is the process to land a new customer in your business?

Chapter 3
✓ What is your game plan to build trust with the people who have the potential to be your best customers?

✓ Where are your existing prospects on the Relationship Curve?

✓ How are you planning to move people along the Relationship Curve?

Chapter 4
✓ What are the 3 Steps to land new customers?

Chapter 5
✓ Have you started a pipeline?

✓ How will you get a commitment from people to one day do business with you?

✓ How are you "Positioned" with the people in your pipeline?

Chapter 6
✓ What do you want to accomplish?

✓ How will you follow up?

Chapter 7
✓ What goals will you set to measure your efforts?

✓ How will you reward yourself?

Chapter 8
✓ Do you inject enthusiasm into all your conversations?

✓ Do you always say what you believe, with a passion and conviction that leaves no doubt?

Chapter 9
✓ Have you prioritized all your pending activities?

✓ What projects have you been meaning to do, but have not found the time for?

✓ Have you completed a project worksheet for each activity you would like to finish?

✓ When will you work on these projects?

Chapter 10

✓ Can you focus exclusively on one activity for a short time?

✓ How will you measure your progress?

Chapter 11

✓ Do you know how to use a call sheet?

✓ How will you increase your cold and warm calling results every week?

Chapter 12

✓ What are you doing to create customer "advocates"?

✓ How will you market into your customer base?

✓ Where can you find more people just like your best customers?

Chapter 13

✓ What traits do your ideal customers share?

✓ How will you find more people just like your best customers?

Chapter 14

✓ Who are the 52 people who most want you to succeed?

✓ Who are the people involved in 'Money in Motion' events in your business?

Chapter 15

✓ How will you introduce yourself to new people?

✓ Have you prepared an introductory script to suit both your product, or service, and you?

✓ Will someone cold call for you?

Chapter 16

✓ What is your qualifying question?

✓ Have you asked this question of everyone in your pipeline?

✓ Are they worth the effort you are going to put into making them your customer?

Chapter 17

✓ Have you promised everyone you would like to meet, that you will not try to sell them anything if they will meet with you?

Chapter 18

✓ Do you have a dynamic ongoing communications program?

✓ When was the last time you sent a hand written note to your best customers?

✓ What have you done lately to help your prospects get to know you better?

Chapter 19

✓ What activities are you doing to meet people?

✓ What networking activities are you part of?

✓ When will your next seminar be?

✓ Who will be your guest speaker?

Chapter 20

✓ Can you think of a networking group theme whose membership would consist exclusively of people just like your best customers?

Chapter 21

✓ Have you created a checklist for your meetings to be sure you are always prepared?

✓ What is your list of important questions that need to be answered for you to know when 'Money will go in Motion'?

Chapter 22

✓ What are the four critical moments that will land the customer every time?

✓ Are you ready to seize the moment?

Chapter 23

✓ Have you completed the Value Proposition worksheet in Appendix 2?

✓ Can you articulate what it is that makes you special?

Chapter 24

✓ Have you built a presentation template that captures everything about you, your company, your product or service, and your value proposition?

✓ Have you practiced your presentation to be sure that it is dynamic, comprehensive, professional and yet easy to understand?

✓ Do you plan to use the "Two Meeting Process" to deliver a powerful presentation?

Chapter 25

✓ How much momentum do you have?

APPENDIX 2

FORMS

DAILY CALL SHEET

NAME: _____ DATE: _____

#	NAME	CALL #	P/V	COMMENTS	ACTION

Doug E. Lachance

WEEKLY CALL SHEET

NAME: _____

WEEK ENDING	CALLS	VISITS	TOTAL PTS*	AVG CALLS PER DAY	TOTAL FIRST CONTACTS
January 7, 2005	86	8	86 + (8x3) = 110	110 ÷ 5 = 22	12 #1's

* Points

Telephone Call: 1 point
Meeting: 3 Points

SAMPLE INTRODUCTORY LETTER
(FOR AN INVESTMENT ADVISOR)

Date

Dear Prospect,

It was a pleasure to speak with you recently. As discussed, I wanted to briefly tell you a little bit about myself, as well as the services I provide. The company I work with is _____

_____

_____

_____

_____

_____.

I believe that the relationship with your investment advisor is probably the single most important ingredient in a successful investment strategy. It is critically important that they have a clear understanding of a client's personality, risk tolerance, objectives, and level of investment knowledge. It is equally important that they have the experience and education to meet those needs. I pride myself in providing the highest level of proactive service and advice, giving clients the strongest advisory asset possible.

I believe strongly in a comprehensive planning process, one that examines the overall 'picture'. After getting to know each other better, we focus on what a person is trying to accomplish (i.e. increased returns/ efficiency in an investment portfolio, tax minimization/planning, retirement, estate, children's education, etc.), and we then quantify those goals. Together, we develop a customized strategy (based on their risk tolerance), specifically designed to meet each person's unique goals and objectives. We meet regularly to review our strategy and evaluate our progress.

Doug E. Lachance

If you should ever have a need, I would be happy to meet with you at your convenience to review any investment advisory needs you may have or to do a complimentary analysis of your financial situation. I value the long-term relationships I have with my clients. I hope that you and I have an opportunity to get to know each other better as time goes along.

"A dream is just a dream. A goal is a dream with a plan and a deadline."
Harvey Mackay

Sincerely,

Your Name
Your Title

SAMPLE CUSTOMER INFORMATION SHEET

Date:_____

NAME:_____

ADDRESS:_____

POSTAL CODE:_____

HOME #:_____

2ND #:_____

BUSINESS #:_____

CELL #:_____

FAX #:_____

EMAIL:_____

SIN:_____

DATE OF BRITH:_____

EMPLOYER:_____

POSITION:_____

TYPE OF BUSINESS:_____

EMPLOYED SINCE:_____

CHEQUE ❑   DRIVERS LICENSE ❑

INCOME:_____

SPOUSE:_____

CHILDREN:_____

SIN:_____

DATE OF BIRTH:_____

SPOUSE EMPLOYEE:_____

INCOME:_____

Doug E. Lachance

ASSETS

NET LIQUID ASSETS:_____

NET FIXED ASSETS:_____

TOTAL:_____

REAL ESTATE:_____

MORTGAGE:_____

WHERE:_____

RENEWAL DATE:_____

FINANCIAL ASSETS

RRSP'S:_____

_____

OTHER INVESTMENTS:_____

_____

INVESTMENT OBJECTIVES

INCOME:_____%

CAPITAL GAINS: RISK FACTORS:

SHORT TERM_____%   LOW_____%

MEDIUM TERM_____%   MEDIUM_____%

LONG TERM_____%   HIGH_____%

COMMENTS:

PERSONAL INFORMATION

WHERE DID YOU GROW UP? _____

SCHOOL? _____

MARRIED? CHILDREN? _____

_____

_____

HOBBIES AND INTERESTS: _____

_____

FAVORITE VACATION SPOT? _____

YOUR HOME? _____

DO YOU ENJOY SEMINARS? _____

WHAT TYPE? _____

_____

WHAT ARE YOUR RETIREMENT GOALS? _____

_____

_____

HOW WOULD YOU LIKE TO BE REMEMBERED_____

_____

_____

MOST IMPORTANT ISSUES? _____

_____

_____

VALUE PROPOSITION WORK SHEET

1) What services do you provide?

2) What qualifications do you have?

3) How do you do what you do?

4) What do you have to offer that is different from your competitors?

5) What makes you special?

6) Why should people want to work with you?

7) How do you add value?

8) What do you promise you will always do for this person?

9) What commitments to this person is part of your service agreement?

10) How often will you communicate with them? When will you be available?

11) What are the costs of doing business with you?

12) Who do you know who would provide a testimonial for you?

ANALYSIS AND PRESENTATION WORKSHEET

ANALYSIS

What tools are available to you to analyze this person situation? Can you add value to this person's life in simply going through the analysis process? If so, whether they are ready to do business today or not you will have given them a reason to see what you could do for them if they were to become your customer

PRESENTATION

The completed presentation should be provided bound with an attractive cover. It should include:

1) **Introduction**—Your introduction should provide an overview of your industry and discuss any "macro" factors that are applicable: the economy, interest rates etc. It should include charts, articles, and any support materials that will outline "the big picture". You will show how you, your company, and your product or service fit within this big picture.

2) **Analysis**—Having used whatever tools you have chosen, now it is the time to share the results. Are this customers needs being met? Is their current program inferior? Why?

3) **Recommendation**—What solutions do you have for them? What is it about your product or service that makes it the perfect choice for them? What are your ideas and strategies that will make them need and want to become your customer?

4) **Corporate and Personal Review** (See Separate Worksheet)—This is where you will show them everything about you and your company that makes you perfect as their provider and the solution to their need or problem.

SEMINAR PLANNING WORKSHEET

1) **Who is your target group?**

   Identify the profile of the people you would like to have attend. (Retirees, business people, executives, professionals, etc)

2) **Choose your topic.**

   Think of one topic or more. A successful concept is to have more than one speaker. Perhaps have an expert on gardening (or other lifestyle topics) and an expert on a business topic (investing for income, tax strategies, RRSP's, etc).

3) **Book the Event.**

   Decide what kind of event you will have and book the room.

   What?—Breakfast; Lunch; Dinner; Coffee and Pastries.
   Where?—Restaurant; Hotel; Boardroom; School; Theatre.
   When?—Choose a date that will give you lots of time to be organized.
   Who?—Book your speakers.

4) **Promotion**

   Invitations; Phone calls; Direct Mail; Advertising; Press Release

5) **Follow up**

   Always confirm attendance a few days before

6) **Be Prepared!**

   Be sure everything you need will be there: Audio-visual equipment; adequate seating; refreshments; door prize(s)

7) **Handout Materials**

   Seminar Packages (marketing materials, speaker handouts); Agenda; Evaluation Questionnaires (It is important to capture the names of attendees. I would ask them to fill out a questionnaire and then, use those to draw the door prize.); Name Tags; Paper and Pencils; Business Cards

SEMINAR EVALUATION QUESTIONNAIRE

Please take a few minutes to critique this seminar to help us make our next seminar better.

1. What is your general impression of this seminar?

   Excellent ❑   Good ❑   Average ❑   Poor ❑

2. Did the seminar cover what you expected? Yes ❑ No ❑

   If no, why not?_____

   _____

   _____

   _____

3. What other seminar topics would interest you?

   1. _____

   2. _____

   3. _____

4. Would you like to receive literature on those or other topics? (specify, if other)

   ❑ Yes   ❑ No

   ❑ Other topics (specify) _____

5. Comments:

Please complete for a chance to win our Door Prize

Name:_____Phone: _____

Address: _____

City:_____ Province: _____Postal Code: _____

PROJECT WORKSHEET

1. Objectives of the Project

Be specific. What is the goal? To arrange presentation opportunities? To meet people? To add new names to your pipeline? To start a networking group?

2. What do you need to do to accomplish this objective?

Perhaps your goal is to arrange 8 presentations per week. Who are you going to call? When are you going to call them? Perhaps your objective is to add 20 new people per week to your pipeline. Once again, whom will you call? When will you call them? You need to figure out whom you want to call and what you want to say to them. Prepare a script.

3. What is your target date to complete?

Is this a one-day project? One week? One month? It is important to set a date to force you to allocate the time and energy to meet this deadline.

4. When will you work on this project?

Now that you know what you want to do, how you're going to do it, and when it needs to be done, you must budget time to get it done. Whether it's an hour set aside, an afternoon, a day, whatever, you must set time aside and when that time comes you must honor this commitment and focus.

5. Monitoring your results.

You started with a stated objective. Are you getting results? If not, why? Do you need to change your script? If you're not having success, something is wrong with the way you're presenting it. Where is the value? Are you expressing it properly?

PROJECT NAME:_____

1. Objectives of the Project

_____

_____

_____

_____

_____

2. What do you need to do to accomplish this objective?

_____

_____

_____

_____

_____

3. What is your target date to complete?

_____

_____

4. When will you work on this project?

_____

_____

5. Monitoring your results.

_____

_____

_____

_____

_____

_____

_____

CORPORATE AND PERSONAL PROFILE WORKSHEET

1. **Organization Profile**
   - Description and History of your company
   - Tools available (in general terms)
   - Product Information (general description of the products and services available from your company)
   - Governing Bodies; Licensing requirements; Continuing Education requirements
   - Discussion of your team and their roles
   - Discussion of Head Office and additional support available
   - Customer Website or other features that make your company special

2. **Personal Profile**
   - Experience and Qualifications
   - Philosophy
   - Commitment and Promises
   - Accomplishments
   - Testimonials

3. **Reporting**
   - Statements
   - Review Process

4. **Communication**
   - Office hours
   - Message Policy
   - Team availability
   - Mailings and other communications (e-mail, newsletters, other publications and information available)

5. **Costs and Fees**
   - Transaction costs and/or management fees
   - Service Fees

SAMPLE LETTER FOR CUSTOMER SURVEYS

Date

Name
Address

Dear XXXXX,

As you know, we take great pride in the level of service we offer. That said, we never want to be complacent. We know that we can make improvements, and the best way to do that is to ask the very best people who do business with us. Please tell us how we are doing by completing the enclosed Evaluation Form.

It will just take a few moments of your time and I assure you that we will diligently review each form.

We know your time is valuable. As a small token of our appreciation, we will donate $X dollars to _____ for every form we receive back from our customers.

Please be candid and, if possible reply by XXXXX. We want to know, as specifically as possible, how you feel about our services, and what is important to you. Your feedback will help us take our services to the next level. We look forward to sharing the results with you in the near future.

If you have any questions about how to complete the form or about some of the questions, we want to help you out—just give XXXX a call.

Sincerely,

Your name
Your Company

P.S. The evaluation can be mailed back in the stamped return envelop or faxed to XXX-XXXX. If you prefer to send your response via email, you may visit our web site at www.XXXXXXX and click on the Evaluation Form link.

SAMPLE SURVEY EVALUATION FORM

1. Name (optional): _____

2. What led you to use our service or product?

   _____

3. Regarding your expectations, have I:
   - ❑ Met
   - ❑ Exceeded
   - ❑ Fallen below

4. What one area would you suggest I work on to improve my level of service?

   _____

   _____

5. What would have to happen over the next 5 years for you to feel this has been a rewarding and meaningful relationship?

   _____

   _____

6. If I were to add new services or products, which would appeal to you the most?
   - ❑   (Fill in with what is applicable for your service or product)
   - ❑
   - ❑
   - ❑
   - ❑

7. Have I *earned the right* for you to refer a friend and family member to me?

   _____

8. Please add any personal comments:

   _____

   _____

THANK YOU FOR YOUR TIME

SAMPLE SURVEY FOLLOW UP LETTER

Date

Name
Address

Dear XXXXX,

Just a quick note to thank my customers for participating in my evaluation survey. As you know, the best way to raise standards of our product or service is to gather feedback from the people who actually receive it. We appreciate your comments.

I have enclosed another evaluation form for your convenience; please disregard it if you have since returned the first. It will take only a few minutes to complete, but I am convinced your time will be well spent. I've already received positive feedback from some of my customers about information I've sent them in response to issues they raised in their questionnaire.

Thank you for your time.

Sincerely,

Your name
Your Company

P.S. The evaluation can be mailed back in the stamp return envelop or faxed to XXX-XXXX. If you prefer to send your response via email, you may visit our web site at www.XXXXXX and click on the Evaluation Form link.

APPENDIX 3

CENTERS OF INFLUENCES—WEBSITES

CENTERS OF INFLUENCES - WEBSITES

Here is a list of websites you may find helpful in locating Centers of Influence.

Lawyers
www.cba.org

Accountants
www.casource.com (The Ultimate Source for C.A.'s)

CFO's
www.cfo.com
www.tmac.ca (Company CFO's and Treasurers)

Insurance
www.cluinstitute.ca

Bankers
www.cba.ca (Canadian Bankers Association)

Notary Publics
www.notaries.bc.ca (BC Society of Notary Publics)

Investment Advisors
See individual firms website.

Real Estate
www.crea.ca (The Canadian Real Estate Association)

Art Dealers
www.ad-ac.ca (The Art Dealers Association of Canada)

SEDAR
www.sedar.com (Information on Public Companies)

SEDI
www.sedi.ca (Disclosure of Information from Insiders)

Financial Planners
www.cafp.org (Canadian Association of Financial Planners

APPENDIX 4

TESTIMONIALS

TESTIMONIALS

I have watched Doug Lachance with amazement over the past 15 years build up two large books of clients in the investment industry...He has a gift of a focus that is second to none. Once Doug gets his goal of gathering clients, just watch him...His organization, focus, discipline and determination is a marvel, and his results are proof positive that it works.

Nancy Shewfelt, Vice President & Director
Wellington West Capital Inc.

'MONEY IN MOTION is an investment advisor's lifetime achievement turned into a simple yet comprehensive recipe book, not just for the investment industry, but the book is applicable to all disciplines, up-and-comers of any industry or business profession.

Benoit Marcotte, Senior Vice President
National Bank Financial

I have just finished reading MONEY IN MOTION for the second time and I think it's great. Perfect for rookies or any advisors looking to jump start a new prospecting campaign. The ideas are there and just need to be put into action. By the way, your strategy of advising prospects that you're not going to try to sell them anything in the first meeting is generating a very positive response.

Dave Robertson, Investment Advisor
ScotiaMcLeod

Doug was my mentor when I came into the business over 20 years ago. He showed me the power of a focused and disciplined work habit and methodology. He was very influential in my formative years and instrumental in helping me become a million dollar producer

Mike Windeler, Investment Advisor, Penticton

Doug E. Lachance

Doug acted as a mentor to me in my all-important first three years as an advisor. He showed me simple but powerful techniques to build my client base and grow my business. Doug's real gift is his ability to cut through the fluff and demonstrate hands on techniques to build ones business. He never said it would be easy but he always helped me stay focused and growing my client base and my business. Now with eight years under my belt, I still use the techniques that Doug taught me and they are as relevant today as they were back then. Quite simply, if you follow Doug's advice you cannot help but to succeed as an advisor. His techniques are neither complicated nor costly. I can honestly say that without Doug's guidance and mentoring I would not have succeeded in those first few crucial years. I would unequivocally recommend Doug to any advisor whatever their experience level.

Brendan Murray
Investment Advisor
ScotiaMcLeod

THE 'MONEY IN MOTION' NATIONAL BANK FINANCIAL WORKSHOP

The following testimonials are taken from Investment Advisors attending the Money in Motion National Bank Financial Workshops.

Your workshop was most useful. It brought back to roost the phrase KISS. It truly is that easy when you just get down to it. The most memorable part that keeps coming back is the need, when calling, to simply want to meet the prospect so you can get to know each other. Your process and methods are easy to follow and I can see them being used by all those who attended.

Jane Drapeau, Manager—Penticton, BC

I found your workshop very worthwhile. By far the most important thing I took from the workshop was the need to make contact with both your clients and your prospects. In fact the next day at our I.A. meeting we developed a branch initiative to submit weekly call sheets that will allow us to track the contact performance of every I.A.—and everyone is committed. This activity alone will bring in a ton of new assets.

Sherman Dahl, Manager—Vernon, BC

Your workshop was a good refresher, but more importantly, your compilation of various aspects of the marketing process is complete. Many of the presentations that I have attended in the past only focus on a certain aspect, leaving the job of organizing all of the bits up to me. Doug you are an entertaining speaker with very interesting stories which makes your presentation very realistic.

Coreen Sol, Manager—Kelowna, BC

I found the workshop of value because it refreshes one's commitment to the need for a formal process to follow on a regular basis. I also found it great because it reinforces the long term, small town way of handling clients and potential clients, namely with respect.

Lance Johnston, Investment Advisor—Penticton, BC

I thought you did a great job. The reference to the system, using call sheets etc. brings back some good old memories. It's a good idea to go back to square one and refresh your self with the prospecting methods that worked well in the past.

Dave Bromley, Investment Advisor - White Rock, BC
National Bank Financial

Listening to Doug Lachance as he reveals the key to successful prospecting is both entertaining and invaluable. Drawing from years of experience and seasoned with a good dose of personal anecdotes, Doug explains the framework and techniques he has found works best. He also identifies resources to draw upon. Anyone who attends the workshop ought to come out motivated and determined to implement a prospecting strategy using many of the tools and methods presented.

Glenn Helminger Investment Advisor, White Rock, BC
National Bank Financial

I liked it. It was a good refresher of some of the basics. I am planning on incorporating a lot of the information contained in you presentation templates in future presentation. I would recommend it.

Paul Borisoff, Investment Advisor—Vancouver, BC
National Bank Financial

THE NBF 'MONEY IN MOTION' ROOKIE TRAINING PROGRAM

The following comments were made by attendees after the NBF Rookie Training Workshop.

This course is probably the single most important of the whole 2 weeks.

Absolutely critical session for asset gathering rookie I.A.'s. Doug was the most charismatic instructor yet!

Great speaker. Created lots of motivation.

Very, very helpful with excellent examples.

Doug's manner, preparation, and expertise are exceptional for this training.

810

London Life, London T-005
HR Training & Education

Money in motion

April 20, 2006

ISBN 141206694-8